Measuring Up 2.0

Measuring Up 2.0

Governing's New, Improved Guide to Performance Measurement
for Geniuses (and Other Public Managers)

JONATHAN WALTERS

THE *GOVERNING* MANAGEMENT SERIES
Governing Books, Washington, DC

Published by *Governing* Books
A Division of *Governing* Magazine
1100 Connecticut Ave., NW, Suite 1300
Washington, DC 20036

www.governing.com

Cover and interior design and composition: Naylor Design, Washington, DC
Cover illustration: David Clark

∞ The paper used in this publication exceeds the requirements of the American
National Standard for Information Sciences—Permanence of Paper for Printed
Library Materials, ANSI Z39.48-1992.

Printed and bound in the United States of America

11   10   09   08   07   1   2   3   4   5

Library of Congress Cataloging-in-Publication Data

Walters, Jonathan
   Measuring up 2.0: governing's new, improved guide to performance measurement
   for geniuses (and other public managers) / Jonathan Walters.—2nd ed.
      p. cm.
   Includes index.
   ISBN 978-0-87289-575-1 (alk. paper)
1. Government productivity—United States—Measurement. 2. Administrative
agencies—United States—Evaluation. 3. State governments—United States—
Evaluation. 4. Local government—United States—Evaluation. I. Title.
   JK2445.P76W33 2007
   352.30973—dc22

                                                                    2007027517

To Pop, wherever he is

Contents

Preface

The first book idea I ever proposed for *Governing* was on Total Quality Management in the public sector. Having just written a feature story for the magazine entitled "The Staying Power of TQM," I was convinced that this was the real thing—a management strategy that was going to transform government into a lean, mean, data-driven machine.

I remember having lunch with the magazine's brain trust (such as it was, given that *I* was there) to talk about the possibility of the magazine getting into the book-publishing business and the possibility that a book on TQM might be the vehicle for launch. Fortunately, we were slow enough and disorganized enough so that by the time we could actually get serious about such an endeavor, TQM had proved its actual staying power and had received an unceremonial burial as a management fad.

More important for me, though: I had learned a valuable lesson about management strategies that come with names. And so when notions like the Balanced Scorecard and Six Sigma came rolling along, I was willing to look at them, but I had the shovel at the ready for the inevitable interment.

But while I became skeptical, I didn't become jaded. In fact, there were some very sound concepts behind techniques like TQM and the Balanced Scorecard. And the one I noticed that wove itself through all these management notions and potions was this: they all tried to get government to focus more tightly and rationally on results.

So when Oregon Benchmarks came along in 1994 (winning an Innovations in American Government Award) it seemed that we were finally getting somewhere. We weren't naming the street anymore, or arguing about the best, most magical method of transportation. We were finally focusing on the destination. Besides Oregon, other jurisdictions seemed to be getting it, too. Worcester, Massachusetts, was pioneering the practice in the mid-1990s. And around the same time, the Governmental Accounting Standards Board was beginning to toy with the concept of "service efforts and accomplishments" reporting (much more on that later), which represented a very general effort to get state and local governments more focused on results.

And so the brain trust, older and wiser, reconvened, and, it being clear that the typical publishers for books about government management were not enthusiastic about one that didn't weigh at least 18 pounds and contain a Library of Congress–worth of footnotes, we decided to self-publish. The result was the first in *Governing*'s growing library of management books, *Measuring Up: Governing's Guide to Performance Measurement for Geniuses (and Other Public Managers)*.

A quick note about the title, which most people think is a play on the *Dummies* book concept. It's not. In my early car-owning days, Volkswagen bugs were de rigueur in my neighborhood, as was working on them yourself. A well-thumbed and greasy copy of *How to Keep Your Volkswagen Alive: A Manual of Step-by-Step Procedures for the Compleat Idiot* became my auto repair bible. The beauty of the book—

besides brilliantly breaking down jobs like a clutch replacement to their essence—was that it was actually fun to read.

So that was my model for *Measuring Up*. There's enough stuffy, complicated, convoluted material out there on performance measurement for long-suffering readers to pore over without my adding to the pile. And it was gratifying to see Ken Miller follow suit with *We Don't Make Widgets*, the most recent offering in the *Governing* Management Series, another very readable book on improving government performance.

In deciding what to include in *Measuring Up 2.0*, I think I'm operating on what is a safe assumption: that the concepts of performance measurement and results-based governance are pretty prevalent. And so, while I do touch on the basics, there's more material in this edition on real-world and more advanced applications, including discussions of the whole "stat" phenomenon, performance-based contracting, comparative measurement consortia, and shorter and more-to-the-point chapters on the fundamentals of—and the inevitable impediments to—implementation. There's also more discussion about the politics of performance measurement, that absolutely unavoidable reality that ultimately drives what government does, even as it drives the poor career schlubs who work in government nuts.

While the book's contents have changed considerably, what I hope most is that it is still at least halfway fun to read, so that when your new elected executive decides to mandate performance-based budgeting for all departments starting this coming fiscal year, I won't actually *add* to your misery.

Besides, as a public official myself, I've learned one thing above all else about serving in government: if you take it too seriously, you're just in for a real bad headache.

Acknowledgments

A big thanks to those who agreed to peruse portions of this book (or the whole thing), including Shelley Metzenbaum (I try to pay her back in homegrown asparagus, but it's never enough), Jay Fountain, Mark Abrahams, and Harry Hatry.

And likewise to the gang at *Governing*, especially Peter Harkness— I'm not sure he actually *read* the first book inasmuch as he was all for me doing a second edition. And especially to my closest partner in crime, my editor John Martin.

Also thanks to Elder Witt and Roger Wilson for their overall support in getting *MU2* on track and finished.

And thanks to the folks at CQ Press for their willingness to break the mold a bit (not the least of which includes allowing me to suggest that the president of the United States and Alfred E. Neuman have more in common than just their good looks)—in particular, Mary Marik and Lorna Notsch for their refreshing enthusiasm.

And last and most, to my bride Eileen Ann, who suffers through all the editorial moodiness that comes with being married to someone whose life is defined by deadlines that respect neither cleaning my bathroom nor romantic (or even pedestrian) dinners out. I promise we'll celebrate your birthday sometime this year.

Jonathan Walters
Ghent, New York

Chapter 1

"Stat"-Happy

When the first edition of *Measuring Up* (*MU1*) came out, the lead anecdote was all about Long Beach, California, and what a mess it was crimewise. In that chapter it was noted that just about everything bad that could be happening to a police department was happening in Long Beach. Evildoers (the local and regional kind, not the international variety) were running amok, making magnificent headway in the push to make Long Beach unlivable. They were running so amok that between 1983 and 1990 crime in general in Long Beach went up by 30 percent; violent crime doubled.

This rapid slide backward snowballed into an unhappy, unhealthy downward trend in recruiting by the Long Beach Police Department: The job was so little fun, and morale at the department was so famously bad, that the city couldn't even fill all of its budgeted staff positions. Nobody wanted to work in a department that was racking up such a lousy string of statistics on such a painfully consistent basis.

As the numbers got worse in Long Beach, the city council began to consider all manner of radical options, including the panacea that continues to be popular in the public sector today when government is faced with some sort of serious, intractable problem: Contract it out. (For more on this phenomenon, see Chapter 7.) In this case, the notion was to turn the job of law enforcement in Long Beach over to the Los Angeles County Sheriff's Department. Hey, if it didn't improve the situation, at least it would allow the city council to blame the county.

In the end, a narrow majority of Long Beach city council members voted against law enforcement by proxy and for fixing the department that they had instead. The foundation for the fix would be to embrace a new trend that had been percolating up in various places all over the country, most notably in New York City. That trend involved a much more sophisticated approach to crime fighting than running around town in a kind of endless tail-chasing exercise where the police were forever trying to deal with crimes *after* they'd occurred, which, timing-wise, isn't particularly helpful to victims.

Instead, Long Beach would begin to fight crime by closely tracking and analyzing crime statistics, patterns, and trends virtually on a daily basis, and it would then begin to deploy resources based on *preventing* crime by dealing with hot spots—an increase of a certain type of offense in a certain part of town at a certain time of day. In New York City, this system was known as "CompStat," which was short for "computer comparison statistics," an absurdly clunky way to say "statistical trend tracking."

Long Beach didn't call its new effort anything "stat" (although "BeachStat" has a nice ring to it). But in essence it was following New York City on the leading edge of a trend that would continue to catch fire—not just in law enforcement but in government generally.

It was the beginning of the stat craze. And if anyone doubts how pervasive a trend it's become, think "IraqStat." That is, when President George W. Bush said an increase in troops came with a demand that the Iraqi government start meeting specific "benchmarks" for performance and progress, he in essence was saying that the United States

CrystalBallStat

An interesting trend on the "stat" front is using data not just to analyze what happened, but to predict what *will* happen and try to prevent it. For a while now, cops, for example, have used time and place mapping as a way to set up stakeouts. But the trend has spilled beyond its obvious applications in law enforcement. The New York City Department of Homeless Services has done an analysis of the neighborhoods in which residents seem most vulnerable to falling into the shelter system. In those neighborhoods, the city is now conducting aggressive outreach through local community service organizations to try to catch people before they fall—they're trying everything from rental assistance to job and marriage counseling. Early evidence is that the preemptive approach to fighting homelessness has promise.

would be looking at data—both practical on-the-ground data and political-progress data—in assessing how open-ended its commitment to the war in Iraq would be. Congress, not incidentally, was demanding the same thing.

Now, there may be those hardened skeptics out there who wonder whether certain high-level, elected officials who bear an amazing resemblance to Alfred E. Neuman (for you youngsters not familiar with the name, Google it and see if you don't agree) are actually capable of responding to real numbers and real news, especially when both are bad.

But we're not going to get bogged down in a discussion of that now. We'll get bogged down in a discussion of that in the last chapter—"Elected Officials: The Weak Link in American Government?" What we will do right now is argue that flying dumb and flying blind are very different things. At least if you've got good data, there is the potential to use that data in making better decisions. If you don't have data at all, then you're just guessing, and in a lot of areas of public policy the stakes are just too high to rely on guessing.

Which brings us back to Long Beach, which had been guessing wrong for too long when it came to crime fighting. Launching its new stat-based battle plan in the late 1990s, the city did, in fact, begin to turn the crime-fighting tide, to wit: In 2003, Long Beach reported 18,613 serious crimes, including 8,074 larcenies/thefts and 50 murders/incidents of manslaughter. In 2004, those numbers were 18,426, 7,436, and 48, respectively. In 2005, they were 17,014, 6,804, and 42. According to the city's 2006 *Report to the Community,* the rate of violent crime per 1,000 residents was 7.44 in 2003. It rose a fraction in 2004 to 7.7, then dipped to under 7 in 2005.

While this may not seem like much of a decline, keep in mind that the numbers had been trending upward for years. Also keep in mind that the gains occurred at a time when most other cities were witnessing *increases* in crime.

After using a results-based approach to crime fighting, Long Beach really caught the stat bug in 2003, says the city's director of communications, Kathy Parsons. She says a projected $102 million budget deficit that year focused the minds of elected officials and public managers in ways previously unseen. "There's been an incredible effort citywide to develop business plans for each department and each bureau within that department," says Parsons. As part of that effort, concrete performance measures have been developed for each bureau.

In 2006, Long Beach published its first *Report to the Community,* which included performance highlights from policy areas ranging from economic development to community health and safety. (To check out the report go to www.longbeach.gov/civica/filebank/blobdload.asp? BlobID=14266.)

In taking the stat approach to governance citywide, Long Beach has become part of a rapidly expanding group of governments that have begun to apply it to governance across a host of policy and program areas.

CompStat on Steroids

Police departments are starting to figure out that as good as time and place mapping of crime might be, there are potentially more powerful ways to use technology and data to fight crime. New York City, for example, has taken CompStat a few steps further by linking numerous databases containing information on everything from an offender's nickname to tattoos as a way to create and follow leads.

Right now, though, it looks like Chicago is leading the high-tech crime-fighting sweepstakes with CLEAR, which stands for "Citizen and Law Enforcement Analysis and Reporting" (state and local government acronyms are more fun than the federal variety, which never spell anything useful).

On the hardware side, CLEAR includes everything from the handheld devices police officers use to both check and collect names, license plates, photos, scars, tattoos, and fingerprints to the mobile cameras that can scan thousands of license plates an hour to check for stolen vehicles or possible fugitives, suspects, or witnesses.

On the intelligence side, CLEAR links databases that offer immediate access to information on everything from arrests and convictions to stolen vehicles, warrants, firearms data, investigative alerts, gang activity, juvenile curfew violations, and incidence reports, among a host of others.

Officially, such operations are coming to be known as "fusion centers," places where large—and rapidly filling—reservoirs of information are stored for quick linked access by law enforcement.

The hallmark of CLEAR is that it allows police to take fragments of information—a partial license plate, a nick-

continued

name, a partial street address—and use those to do a full-blown database search to see if the information matches up with a solid name and address or other lead. With CLEAR it can be just about any detail related to a crime or a suspect. For example, in one recent case the Chicago PD had only a discarded lottery ticket as evidence at a murder scene. Guessing the number on the ticket might have some significance, they ran it as a street address through CLEAR, got a clean hit on a career criminal, cross-checked DNA found at the scene with samples on file, and made the arrest.

CLEAR also has worked in a powerful community component. Just for starters, it allows citizens to quickly find out who, exactly, is policing their neighborhoods, from foot patrols to beat commanders. And it allows for the rapid exchange of information on crime and criminal activity in specific neighborhoods.

Currently, 20,000 citizens and local businesspeople subscribe to a service through CLEAR that offers regular updates on what's going on in specific beats (there are 280 citywide, generally organized along the lines of recognized neighborhoods), including alerts if police are seeing—or anticipate—some uptick in criminal activity in a particular area, or if they need help finding a particular person. CLEAR also allows citizens to pull up maps of crime activity in their neighborhoods.

As of this writing, the department was also working on a way to text-message interested community members about any alerts, bulletins, upticks in gang and criminal activity, and the like in their neighborhoods.

City officials credit the system for Chicago's steady drop in property and violent crime since 2003, even as other major cities have witnessed increases.

Taking Stat Citywide

It didn't take long for astute observers of public management to notice what was happening in places like New York City and Long Beach on the crime-fighting front, and to think about what could be accomplished in other tough policy areas if officials shifted their gaze from measuring and monitoring activity to measuring and monitoring results.

If it could work in policing, thought some enterprising public officials, then why not domestic violence prevention (SpatStat), truancy (BratStat), building inspections (FireTrapStat), environmental protection (SpillStat), economic development (GovGiveawayStat), garbage collection (StinkStat), libraries (CatInTheHatStat), pest control (RatStat), or even childhood obesity (FatStat)?

And so from the late 1990s through to today, a number of cities—and at least two states—have decided that the stat approach to governing could be broadened to virtually every area of public policy and administration.

The first big expansion of stat-happiness occurred in 2000 in Baltimore, when Mayor Martin O'Malley (now *Governor* Martin O'Malley of Maryland, it's worth noting) decided to manage the whole city on a stat basis. Every two weeks he would haul his department heads and their top staff in and demand progress reports in areas ranging from crime fighting to cleaning up vacant lots.

As Christopher Swope describes in a penetrating and prescient *Governing* feature story (www.governing.com/archive/2001/apr/omalley. txt) on the new mayor's arguably quixotic attempt to turn a very tough city around, O'Malley's goal in pushing CitiStat was as much about the city's overall well-being as it was an attempt to transform the government bureaucracy running the place. O'Malley figured that to perform better as a government, the bureaucracy needed a shake-up, and the vehicle for that shake-up was reality, whether it was in the specific area of restaurant inspections or parks and recreation.

And while many upper-level bureaucrats felt beset-upon by a cranky, impatient mayor, the more enlightened ones quickly realized that it was an opportunity to make their case. If things weren't going great, after all, it might be on account of a lack of resources, or it might be on account of something within the municipal operating environment that was getting in the way of getting the job done, such as dumb procurement or personnel rules. Besides, it wasn't as though O'Malley hadn't stepped up on the stat front himself. In fact, part of his platform when he first ran for mayor was a pledge to get the city's infamously high murder tally below 300 a year (something he accomplished in his first year).

Within a few years of launching CitiStat, Baltimore had made some interesting progress in areas large and small. Not only did violent crime come down, but potholes were being filled faster, towing of abandoned vehicles increased 22 percent, the amount of graffiti removal blossomed fourfold, and lead-abatement efforts expanded significantly. More broadly, the economy of the city appeared to improve—at least by one key measure, private sector employment, which went up. And it was through the stat process that the city made such historic discoveries as this: Baltimore was employing probably the last municipal blacksmith in the country (he was forging special tools for the public works department). It was just one of numerous areas in which the city uncovered anachronistic practices that were getting in the way of efficient performance.

Now, Baltimore hasn't transformed itself into Orlando or Sunnyvale or Charlotte thanks to CitiStat. Anyone who has roamed its tougher neighborhoods knows that Baltimore isn't going to be remade, overnight, into some troublefree garden spot because it's started to do a more sophisticated job of tracking and reporting data. As this book will argue consistently, performance measurement and management isn't some magical potion, like Botox, that will wipe away the wrinkles and scars in one easy, painless treatment.

What it does, though, is allow you to better manage people and money, which is especially important in a tough environment like Baltimore. And the city did, in fact, start to get a real handle on all the tough issues it was facing, and it did start to more methodically tackle them.

And that's the real story. Performance measurement and management allows a city or state to focus more tightly and rationally on what's happening on the ground—on cause and effect. It doesn't, however, make problems automatically disappear.

A final testimony to the value of CitiStat is that it more than survived its first run-in with political transition, which is usually a sure guillotine for high-level management initiatives in government. Rather than rename, rescind, or otherwise try to erase a notable success achieved by a predecessor, O'Malley's mayoral successor, Sheila Dixon, has actually embraced and expanded CitiStat (see http://baltimorecity. gov/news/citistat/index.html). Not only that, a few weeks after Philadelphia's 2007 mayoral primary, Dixon entertained a visitor: Philly's Democratic mayoral nominee, Michael Nutter, making a pilgrimage to Baltimore to check out CitiStat. Whereas the administration of Philadelphia Mayor John Street (whom Nutter was destined to replace barring a sudden influx of hundreds of thousands of Republicans into Philly before the November election) has expressed some reservations about the perils of raising expectations when it comes to city services (see 3-1-1 sidebar, page 11), Nutter is apparently of the opinion that one core function of city government—besides chasing conventions, building millionaires new sports stadiums, and begging for federal money—is to provide service.

WindyCitiStat

For all their potential benefits, "GovStats" of any type can be complicated and tricky to implement. Chicago is one of the most recent entrants into the stat sweepstakes, and as Ron Huberman, Mayor Richard M. Daley's former chief of staff (now president of the city transit system), will readily admit, it's been an interesting and occasionally messy experiment. While upper and middle management seem to be on board, Huberman notes that the rank and file haven't exactly embraced the notion. (This may be in part because of how Chicago is using some of the data, which we'll get into in Chapter 2, "Crime and Punishment.")

Obstacles or no, Chicago has launched Chicago Performance Management (CPM), or what the stat-happy might call "ChiStat" or how about "GoStat." Actually, Chicago already had a reputation as a pretty well-run city. Mayor Daley comes from that generation of municipal leaders who believe that good management is good politics, and so he has placed a premium on finding talented people to work in high-level positions in Chicago and then cut them loose to perform (this is what's coming to be known as "the Bloomberg model," after New York City Mayor Michael Bloomberg, one of the most expert practitioners of the "find good people, set clear goals, cut them loose, and back them up" school of public management).

Like any good politician-administrator, Daley's reasons for launching CPM were partly political and partly administrative. The city had been squeezed for the preceding few years by a nepotism scandal that was inching ever upward, toward the mayor's office. (Why people get excited about possible nepotism in Chicago is something of a mystery. It's akin to being shocked to learn that certain 1,800-pound NFL linemen have tested positive for steroids and human growth hormones.) But as federal indictments began climbing up the chain of command, it was only natural that the mayor respond somehow to deflect attention. Which also helps explain why CPM includes not only a citywide push on performance measurement and management, but also "a compliance component housed in the [city's] Department of Law, that will ... ensure departments are complying with City policies."

Fig leaf or not, the city has begun measuring with a vengeance across a host of internal and outside services. For example, fleet management began to be scored not on the number of oily rags lying around the shop but on actual "vehicle availability." Streets and Sanitation began tracking everything from tree trimming to timely streetlight repair and replacement. Both water-meter reading and graffiti removal are monitored for productivity gains. The Department of Transportation started tracking potholes that are reported through the city's 3-1-1 system and how quickly they were repaired along the city's 3,789 miles of roadways and 1,900 miles of alleys.

The Magic of 3-1-1, or Letting Stats Come to You

There was a time when 9-1-1 was the number of choice for citizens who wanted to report everything from a murder in progress to failure of the local Department of Public Works to pick up the trash that week. As you can imagine, the latter type of 9-1-1 calls weren't really helpful when it came to efficient, effective emergency management and response.

And so a number of cities—including Chicago; New York; Baltimore; Des Moines; Houston; Lexington, Kentucky; and Somerville, Massachusetts—kicked off 3-1-1 programs (in Washington State, Governor Christine Gregoire is thinking about a statewide 3-1-1 system).

The rationale for doing 3-1-1 is fourfold. First, it diverts nonemergency calls out of the 9-1-1 stream (New York City reports that it was able to considerably scale back on its 9-1-1 dispatchers as 3-1-1 took root). Second, it provides citizens with a one-stop call center for all sorts of other issues, from requests for information about local farmers' markets, to reporting hazardous pavement conditions, to queries about whether there really are giant octopuses living in the city's sewer system.

Third, and perhaps most interesting, 3-1-1 systems have become a kind of organic gauge of what is going on out in the community, what is bothering people, what they care about, and what issues cities seem to be dealing with over and over (or not at all).

And so 3-1-1 evolved into kind of an ongoing citizen survey of concerns and of government performance. Cities from Olympia, Washington, to Clearwater, Florida, also offer sites on city Web pages where citizens can file queries, complaints, and requests for service. In Clearwater, it's called the Citizen Issue Tracking System. "It was actually developed in-house

continued

by our own IT staff," says city communications director Doug Matthews. Each substantive query gets a "ticket number," and action is tracked as those queries work their way through the city bureaucracy.

Which is the fourth way in which 3-1-1 and its Web-based ilk are being used: as a management tool. As in Clearwater, comments or complaints that require city follow-up are typically assigned tracking numbers, and action on the calls is traced to gauge how well the city does in responding. In Clearwater, citizens who go the Web route are actually sent updates along the way as a job ticket works its way through the system and, hopefully, to its resolution. (To check out the Clearwater system, go to www.clearwater-fl.com/services/cits/index.asp.) Some cities even do random follow-ups with the citizens to ensure that a problem was taken care of.

The downside to 3-1-1 systems? They can be expensive to build and maintain. New York City, for example, spends millions of dollars a year on its system, which employs hundreds of operators—operators who, not incidentally, have to be of enough different nationalities to be fluent in dozens of languages.

3-1-1 systems can have one other distinct disadvantage, as well, as was expressed last spring by Philadelphia mayor John Street's chief of staff, Joyce Wilkerson. In discussing the possibility of Philly installing 3-1-1, Wilkerson told a *Philadelphia Inquirer* reporter: "People don't want to just complain, they want results. You have to make sure you have the capacity to service the request. You have to have the money in the budget to fill potholes; the department needs enough people to go out and do the work."

In other words, you have to be careful with this 3-1-1 business, because people might, by god, start actually expecting service!

Nor has the city shied away from tougher-to-measure areas such as human services. For example, the city used to track the number of emergency food boxes it was giving out annually—a rather blunt instrument for measuring the overall health and well-being of city residents (their hunger quotient, specifically). In 2006, the city started tracking how often a person or family *returned* to pick up a food box. The city then focused on repeat users, assigning each one a caseworker to help the client with job training and placement. After one year, food-box distribution dropped dramatically—by more than 70 percent—while the number of families in case management doubled. City officials also credit the new focus on self-sufficiency and permanence with a 270 percent increase in job placements made by case managers working with public-housing residents.

Clearly, a host of factors have contributed to those kinds of numbers, not the least of which has been Chicago's generally healthy economy and the recent success of its professional baseball and football teams (just kidding). Just as clearly, though, such ultimate goals as "permanent" job placements or even more ambitious goals such as "self-sufficiency" can be determined only by extensive and long-range study. It's one thing to get people into jobs; it's quite another to shepherd them into positions where they're finally making it on their own with no outside help. But from the standpoint of "interim" measures—that is, concrete markers that one could argue reliably indicate progress—the human services numbers coming out of Chicago are worth noting.

Is CitiStat magic? In truth, lots of exigencies influence a city's performance, including regional economic trends, the weather, and, of absolutely paramount importance, where *Money* magazine ranks you in its "Best Places to Live" issue. (In fact, a separate rankings tome, *Cities Ranked & Rated,* recently put Modesto, California, at the bottom of its list of 375 metro areas, which makes sense; otherwise it would be called "Exemplaresto, California." For a more thorough send-up of the municipal ratings game, see www.governing.com/archive/1995/sep/rate.txt.)

But it's unlikely that perennial rankings and ratings cellar-dwellers like Waterbury, Connecticut, and Yuba City, California, are suddenly going to become economically spectacular and socially glamorous places to live by enacting "YubaStat" or "BuryStat" (actually, given that Waterbury is a well-recognized training ground for future corrupt Connecticut politicians, perhaps "GraftStat" might be a helpful step in a better municipal direction).

Buffalo, New York, for example, is one of the latest entrants into stat-happiness with, logically enough, "CitiStat Buffalo" (although Larisa Benson, who runs Washington State's stat program, makes what I think is a good argument for "BuffStat").

Now, given that what gets measured most frequently in Buffalo is snow depth, bringing attention to Queen City metrics might seem a tad risky. Still, there are signs of life along the old Erie Canal. According to a 2007 article written for the *New York Real Estate Journal*, Buffalo is "experiencing a development boom not seen in decades." The fact that the article was written by Buffalo Mayor Byron Brown might suggest a certain bias, but it appears that Mayor Brown is serious about pushing for a Buffalo comeback. And while it may seem crazy for the mayor of a city famous for decline to start measuring progress, you have to admit the guy has guts.

StateStat

Given the growing popularity of stat-based municipal government, it's only logical that a state would take notice and give it a shot. And it's not much of a surprise that the state that chose to do that first is Washington. That's because, of all the states, Washington was one of the earliest to look seriously at performance measurement when it was led by two-term Governor Gary Locke, a pragmatic politician with a flare for management.

While a certain current governor of Washington hasn't exactly bent over backward to assign credit where it's due, the fact is that Locke created a bureaucratic culture in the state of Washington that began seriously shifting the focus of government from measuring activities to considering results.

To current Governor Christine Gregoire's credit, though, she has stepped up and added some high-level pop to the change in approach through the creation of "GMAP," short for "Government Management Accountability and Performance." Basically GMAP is "WashStat," an effort to measure everything from the time it takes to respond to complaints of child abuse and neglect to the time it takes to clear accidents off of Washington highways.

According to data provided by the governor's office, the state has made interesting progress in everything from job placement of welfare recipients to a reduction of workplace injuries in key areas of employment such as construction. More interesting, though, GMAP has allowed the state to do some disaggregation—that is, to compare the performance of one part of the state with another part to see if any lessons can be learned from studying a high-performing area or unit.

For example, in analyzing the numbers on how quickly the state was responding to reports of child abuse, one region was clearly lagging behind. What's interesting is what the state didn't and did do about it. What it didn't do was threaten every worker in the poorly performing region with summary disciplinary action and/or dismissal if things didn't get turned around in the region and fast. What the state did do was analyze caseloads on a region-by-region basis, and it discovered rather quickly that caseloads in the laggard region were much higher than in other parts of the state.

State officials did two things at that point. They worked on reassigning caseworkers to even things up statewide. But the state also laid down a very public and clearly stated goal: that the state would improve its rate of responding to reports of abuse and neglect within 24 hours from 75 percent of the time to 90 percent. It took some time and some reconfiguring of staffing in regional offices, but by the end of 2006, the state was reporting that it had achieved its goal of child protective services workers responding to 90 percent of emergency abuse complaints within 24 hours, seven days a week. According to the report, "Of course, the ultimate goal is 100 percent, but this interim standard was a critical first step."

It's interesting to note, says Larisa Benson, the GMAP coordinator, that the state initially tackled the problem by *reassigning* staff—she says the state legislature had too little confidence in the state's social services department to actually add new staff to help ease caseloads. The state's most recent budget, by contrast, includes funding for around 50 new protective services worker positions, a direct result, thinks Benson, of a new GMAP-driven confidence in the department.

Sometimes, though, the mere act of statistical comparison can light a little fire under an agency. According to GMAP staff, a county-by-county analysis of job placements by social services staff showed one county in particular—Pierce—lagged way behind. After that less-than-stellar performance was highlighted (GMAP meetings are open to everyone, including the press), staff in that county decided to do a statistical analysis of which of its employment services contractors were the most helpful in getting people jobs. Acting on its findings, the county began shifting resources to the job-placement programs that were getting the best results. After just four months of pursuing the new investment strategy, Pierce County was reporting a 100 per-cent increase in placements. Officials are now trying to roll out the Pierce County method in other parts of the state.

Nor is GMAP meant to push performance in a bureaucratic vacu-um, says Benson. The purpose of GMAP is to focus on higher-level goals, such as employment and child welfare, and then figure out which departments have some piece of that goal. And so officials are brought in to GMAP meetings not on an agency-by-agency basis, but on the basis of the high-level goal at hand. "Then we drill down at the agency level to see what indicators might apply," says Benson.

The question for Washington now is whether GMAP can maintain its momentum. Key to "stat" success is that some high-level person with clear authority (mayors and governors are good; short of that, a designated lieutenant who everyone knows has real power works, too) attend all meetings. As long as Gregoire doesn't resort to "fly-bys"—that is, sitting in at the start of the GMAP sessions but leaving (which sends a less-than-forceful message to the troops when it comes to executive commitment)—then GMAP should be okay.

Meanwhile, back on the East Coast, politically upwardly mobile Maryland Governor O'Malley has officially brought CitiStat to Annapolis as "StateStat," an effort that some argue might also be called "USSenateStat," or maybe even "PrezStat," given O'Malley's likely political ambitions.

Follow-up: For quite a thorough treatise on the mechanics of stat-style programs, see Mark Abramson and Bob Behn's article, "The Varieties of CitiStat," in the May/June 2006 *Public Administration Review*, and Behn's recently published report for the IBM Center for the Business of Government available now at www.businessofgovernment. org/main/publications/index.asp.

Whether at the city or state level, the stat craze clearly has legs right now (although a variant on stat called "dashboards" is beginning to

---

To Dash or Not to Dash

A semi-new twist on presenting performance data is the "dashboard" (OK, it's not new at all, but it seems just now to be catching on in wider circles).

The idea behind a dashboard is to take sets of key measures and illustrate them in color-coded graphics as a way to quickly flag areas in which your shop is either doing well (green), could use some improvement (yellow), or is flunking the performance measurement test (red).

In theory, dashboards make performance measures instantly meaningful because they quickly allow policymakers and managers and budgeters to focus their attention on areas of need, without having to pore through actual data on performance. Critics of dashboards think they're too blunt an instrument for the often delicate job of gauging performance, and that the real story is in the rawer information.

---

continued

Some places have found a way to combine the two. The Chicago Police Department, for example, uses a dashboard-style system to track things like excessive-use-of-force complaints against police officers, along with other things like officers' use of sick time. A simple spreadsheet with real data about an officer's performance will automatically turn up a particular category in need of some attention—in either yellow or red if there's something out of kilter. Any cop who's in yellow may get called in for a chat about performance; red and it's a sure bet.

pop up, too; dashboards use much flashier graphics to illustrate the data's message). And if more politicians like O'Malley and Daley prove that stat can advance them politically—or at least help keep federal prosecutors at bay—then stat-happiness is likely to continue spreading across the land. In fact, there is now something like the equivalent of "WorldStat" popping up in the form of the Community Indicators Consortium (www.communityindicators.net/about.html), the goal of which is to highlight and promote places that are using stat-like measures to gauge general community well-being globally. Sure it's a big job, but, hey, if Buffalo can do it, why not Bangkok?

Crime and Punishment— "GotchaStat!"

I n *MU1*, Chapter 2 was devoted to all the reasons expert bureaucratic roadblockers will use to thwart the introduction of a performance measurement program like a "citistat" or a "statestat." There were seven of them and the chapter was a reader favorite, so it hasn't been ditched entirely in *MU2*; it is condensed below.

But in the course of watching performance measurement efforts come and go and crash and burn since *MU1* came out, and in talking to world-class experts on the subject of how to use performance measurement data to manage and motivate, it has become increasingly clear that the most powerful and pervasive enemy of performance measurement is fear. People in the trenches and in middle management just naturally figure that if higher-ups are going to start quantifying performance, the data will be used first and foremost to beat them black and blue.

And so the second half of this chapter will be given over to the performance measurement imperative: that it be powerfully and consistently communicated to everyone involved that data will not be used to punish people, but to stimulate discussion about what's going right and what isn't and why. (It ought to be that simple, but it never is. The human management and parental impulses are always to reward and punish. If somehow we could just get folks to start using information on results to do a little straightforward analysis rather than as a carrot or a stick, the world would be a better place.)

Crime ...

But before we get into all that, a rehash of the Big Seven—why performance measurement won't work in your world:

Reason Number 1: We already did that.

Well, not exactly.

First you did Program Planning Budgeting. Next you did Zero-Based Budgeting. Then you did Management by Objectives. Then you ginned up your Total Quality Management teams. Six Sigma came and went without you ever getting even your green belt. The Balanced Scorecard hit you and, well, knocked you off balance (no black belt for you). But here's the interesting thing about each of these management panaceas: They all depended on your knowing something about what it was you (or your department or agency or unit) were supposed to be accomplishing. Sound familiar?

Reason Number 2: Performance measures are inherently unfair because I only have so much actual control over outcomes.

This is a tough nut to crack, of course, because so much of what government is trying to accomplish depends on the peskiest of all variables: human behavior. If only Bill Gates could get that chip lodged into the base of our skulls, the one that would turn us into law-abiding, Excel-spreadsheet-using, virus-free do-gooders who while away our hours either (a) working, (b) ordering things on the Web, or (c) contributing to our favorite philanthropy, everything would be fine.

The related complication is that, in areas where government is trying to get stuff done that involves human behavior, it can be tough to make the correlation between government action and bankable results. Was it the job-training program that helped get Jack or Jane off of welfare, or was it the fact that benefits were time-limited? Was it a bit of both? Did the error rate in state tax returns improve because forms got simpler or because the threat of penalties for messing up got worse?

The connection gets even harder to make when one considers that the ultimate results of many government actions won't be known for a long time. After all, the real measure of success for children who've spent 12 years in public school is that they grow up to be happy, fulfilled, and law-abiding adults *without* having to have that chip implanted at the base of the skull.

The cause-and-effect and long-term-consequences conundrums of performance measurement are two of the clubs with which its critics most frequently and happily beat it up. (The other club is the apples-versus-oranges argument, which we'll get to in a bit.)

But as discussed in *MU1*, more and more public officials are dismissing the argument that in the face of such unknowables and such unanswerables as those surrounding cause and effect, the best thing to do is to forget about all this performance measurement hooey. In fact, they're arguing that we're way past due forging ahead—that it's about time government started getting serious about gathering performance data so that some long-term analyses of cause and effect can finally begin.

Take the whole area of corrections, a policy field that was presented as one of the most resistant to the performance measurement ethic as it was breaking over government, in part because of the politics of criminal justice but also on account of the very human side of crime and criminals, good and evil, and what it takes to get people to behave.

Not long ago, performance in corrections pretty much was judged by a single measure: Did any inmate initiate a personal "early" release—absent official approval by the proper authorities? Today, though, the approach seems to be a bit more sophisticated. As Alan

Greenblatt outlines in a March 2007 feature story in *Governing* (www.
governing.com/archive/2007/mar/prisons.txt), corrections officials
and those who make the laws impacting criminal justice policy are
finally figuring out that recidivism rates actually matter. What inspired this new, soft-hearted approach to crime and criminals? A
hard-headed look at the cost of warehousing offenders, dumping
them back on the street with little or no preparation for re-entering
civil society, and then having them come back.

Joe Fistrovich, who currently does health and human services budgeting in Indiana but who became addicted to performance measures
while helping run the state's corrections system, says he noticed something interesting happen after he started measuring some very basic
administrative things such as food costs per facility. Some of his program people also got interested in performance measurement. His
juvenile justice guy, for example, started wondering which of the
many programs for troubled youth that the state was offering seemed
to have the greatest power to reduce recidivism, so he started trying to
make a correlation.

And when the officials who deal with homelessness in New York City
began disaggregating the numbers behind their client base, they discovered that their number one category of regular customer was recently
released prisoners. That type of measurement, and then follow-up
analysis, led to a whole new push for improving release protocols that
involved a host of players—from advocates for the homeless, to state
and city corrections officials, to local advocacy groups, and even to
neighborhood business groups. Again, the idea is to prep the perp before dumping the poor soul on the street.

Will such efforts pay off? Well, it may take a while before we find
out for certain. But it sure is worth tracking.

Reason Number 3: Performance measurement is going to invite unfair comparison.

Ahh, apples versus oranges, otherwise known as "the great fruit-salad
debate." We will get into this more thoroughly in Chapter 6, on comparative measurement consortia. But here's the short course: It is impor-

tant to recognize what will very likely be a high-profile consequence of broad performance measurement efforts nationwide. As governments and government agencies start to collect performance data, the performance of those governments and government agencies is going to start being compared from one jurisdiction to the next whether they like it or not.

People may ask, for example, why the murder rate went down in Los Angeles in 2006, while in Boston it edged up (or, if you really want to get into it, why it went up like a bottle rocket in New Orleans in the same period). One need only watch the recriminations fly after *Money* magazine publishes its aforementioned goofy but widely circulated "Best Places to Live" issue each year to know how sensitive public officials are to high-visibility comparisons.

There are three separate branches of the apples versus oranges (and also versus grapes) debate. The first is that it is unfair to compare the performance of places that are just plain socioeconomically different. The second is that it is unfair to compare the performance of places that are basically different for reasons of administrative operating environment (unions versus no unions, for instance) or actual environment (snow versus no snow). The third is that different jurisdictions may do their measuring differently, and so one might end up looking better than another only because of the way a certain outcome is defined and not because of actual performance.

In fact, well-designed performance measurement efforts embrace comparison, and they invite informed discussion about jurisdictional differences in performance. Why did L.A.'s murder rate nose down while Boston's edged up? Searching for an answer to that question could tell both cities something about fighting violent crime. And in fact, and much to their credit, Boston officials have been working hard to answer that question—an effort directly aimed at analyzing potential reasons for the upturn.

The fact is, once a critical mass of jurisdictions begins to produce half-decent statistics measuring performance in certain key areas—whether it's internal administration or law enforcement, social services delivery or education—the comparisons are going to start flying anyway. They already are. Such issues as who has the most effective welfare-to-work programs, the smartest kids, the best cops, the fastest snowplows, the cleanest drinking water, and so forth are of intense interest to citizens. And so enlightened jurisdictions are jumping into the comparison game preemptively because there are few better motivators out there (speaking of human behavior) than a little competition.

Reason Number 4: Performance measurement is a great idea, but what happens when this administration gets tossed out of office?

Anyone who has spent any time in or around government understands the famous bureaucratic principle known as the "B" rule. That is, career staff will "be" there when the new and ambitious administration sweeps in, and they'll still "be" there when that administration is swept out.

And so it's hard to get longtime career staff excited about the incoming newly elected executive's promise to use the Japanese *kaizan* approach to continuous improvement to help everyone in government do more with less (what a tantalizing prospect!). Many hardened trench dwellers are more inclined to believe that the new executive in question is less interested in weird foreign words than in their own continuous political improvement (see "O'Malley, Martin" and "Giuliani, Rudy").

Let's face it, political timelines and temperaments can foment against serious, long-lasting performance measurement efforts—or any other management trend, for that matter. But while politics will certainly continue to be one of the principal reasons why performance measurement doesn't fly in a lot of places, it is also one of the big reasons why it *does* fly in others.

Performance measurement *can* make good political sense. Just ask Richard Daley in Chicago. Or take Rudy Giuliani. Arguably his political career was catapulted upward by his (and his city's) response to 9/11. But Giuliani had already built a strong platform from which to launch by picking up where his mayoral predecessor, David Dinkins, had left off, emphasizing performance on such basics as street safety (including adding police), graffiti removal, overall city cleanliness, and so forth, all of which were closely monitored through the city's well-known *Mayor's Management Report* (the latest version of which can be found at http://home2.nyc.gov/html/ops/html/mmr/mmr. shtml).

Still, the larger problem of the politician's role in performance measurement can't be dismissed, and we'll get into that more in Chapter 8. Many elected officials—particularly state and local legislators—don't really understand performance measurement, and that represents a serious long-term impediment to effective implementation.

State after state—from Texas to Maine—has passed legislation requiring "performance-based budgeting," or some reasonable facsimile thereof. But look at budgets from those states and you'll notice that what really drives budgeting is that all-important and central variable that seems to drive everybody's budget: How much did we get last year?

Reason Number 5: There's no way to measure what I do.

This is why, as with *MU1*, an entire chapter (Chapter 4) of this book is devoted to answering this most common argument against performance measurement in the public sector. But, as Ken Miller notes in *We Don't Make Widgets* (*Governing* Books, 2006), when you really look dispassionately at what government does, quite a lot of it lends itself very directly to being measured. Meanwhile, there are those hard-nosed types out there who will argue quite eloquently that if you can't measure what you do—such as kids who are better off, or miles of snowy pavement well plowed, or driver's licenses accurately and legitimately issued in a reasonable amount of time—then maybe you should think about a change in vocation.

Reason Number 6: My agency (or department or division) has conflicting missions.

There *are* agencies that seem to suffer from bipolar disease. In *MU1*, we discussed the U.S. Department of the Interior as an example. Its job is to accommodate snowmobilers in Yellowstone, on the one hand,

and protect napping grizzlies, on the other. But so few agencies are in this category that we're going to officially de-list conflicting mission as a recognized reason for opposing performance measures. Pick another number.

Reason Number 7: I still don't feel like it.

As mentioned in *MU1*, some form of prolonged performance measurement filibuster will probably ultimately work if there is a critical mass of resistance to the idea in your department, division, or whatever. It's unlikely that U.S. Speaker of the House Nancy Pelosi and Senate Majority Leader Harry Reid are going to scold your agency for failure to GPRA-itize your budget (that's Government Performance Results Act, in case you really haven't felt like knowing). George W. Bush won't call in an air strike on your office building because you failed to complete a strategic plan (unless there's clear evidence of the existence of WMD). Scooter Libby won't leak your spouse's name to *Congressional Quarterly* as being an extra on *Gilmore Girls* because you ignored the dictates of the Office of Management and Budget's "Program Assessment Rating Tool." Nor are state and local government career staff unfamiliar with the strategy of running out the political clock on the latest management fad.

But *MU2* will pick up where *MU1* left off and continue to argue that there's a less cynical way to view and approach performance measurement, and that is to figure out what it might be able to do *for* you, rather than *to* you.

Some people are actually using the momentum of performance measurement to get more funding for their agencies, to win some flexibility from dumb rules and regulations, to streamline overall operations, or to simply run their shops in a more efficient and effective way because that makes their work lives more satisfying. Oh, and also to illustrate that they know what they're doing.

Carol McFarland, who collects and coordinates performance data for the Oklahoma Health Care Authority, says a significant reason for expanding Medicaid coverage in Oklahoma was to try to train low-income Oklahomans away from resource-draining emergency-room visits. When a special task force looking into the state's medical system flagged emergency-room visits as a key concern, McFarland's shop was ready with not only specific numbers about emergency-room use by Medicaid recipients but also the authority's plan to key in on chronic users as a way to reduce costs. "That came up as a concern, and we were able to show that we were on top of it," says McFarland.

... and Punishment

As mentioned at the very beginning of this chapter, you might be reluctant to embark on a performance measurement effort for yet another reason: that a poor showing will only add up to public ridicule, punishment, and humiliation. In other words, all the responses to bad news or poor performance at which non-genius public sector managers are so very adept.

To wit: In describing Chicago's stat effort at a *Governing* conference about managing performance, Ron Huberman, who directed the effort while he was Mayor Daley's chief of staff, got into some details about how it worked. For example, Huberman discussed the city's tow-truck drivers and their treatment and disposition under the new performance management regime. The high-performing ones got all the newest and best trucks with such amenities as working radios, heat, cup holders, and "naked-lady-in-recline" air fresheners hanging from the rear-view mirrors (actually, I made the air-freshener part up). All the poor performers got the oldest, most beat-up trucks (I didn't make that up).

Now, I don't know what the other geniuses in the room were thinking when he said that, but here's what I was thinking: "Why be so generous with the poor performers? Why let them keep any truck at all? Why not give them an old mountain bike and a length of rope? That'd *really* show 'em!"

Well, to Huberman's credit, he did acknowledge a couple of things: first, that the city's rank and file weren't totally on board when it came to this new measurement stuff (what a surprise) and, second, that measuring a tow-truck driver's performance wasn't a cut-and-dried thing.

When he made the latter observation, I realized that there was hope for Chicago's performance measurement program. Measuring performance in any program or policy area is *rarely* a cut-and-dried thing, which is the main reason why data on performance should not be used to beat people up—at least not initially.

Performance measurement whiz and guru Shelley H. Metzenbaum is eloquent on the subject of "de-motivating" public sector employees and sabotaging performance measurement efforts by using data to punish people. As she points out in discussing seminal and long-lasting performance measurement efforts such as New York City's CompStat, which got started under Bill Bratton (who is currently making some very interesting progress in implementing CompStat as police chief in Los Angeles): "Bill Bratton never got upset with people for bad numbers. He got upset with people when they couldn't explain *why* the numbers were bad or if they didn't have a plan for turning things around." (For a great treatise on how to use performance measures constructively, see Metzenbaum's IBM Center for the Business of Government report, *Performance Accountability: The Five Building Blocks and Six Essential Practices,* available electronically at www. businessofgovernment.org/pdfs/MetzenbaumReport2.pdf.)

Ken Miller hits the same note in *We Don't Make Widgets* in discussing (ridiculing is more like it) another goofy management concept that won't die: pay for performance. In a high-stress environment where people are being asked to do extraordinary things—such as finding troubled kids good homes (or just getting them out of really bad ones), or keeping rush hour rolling around big cities, or maintaining the health of our environment—drilling (or rewarding) one or two or a handful of people for some area of public sector performance can be a pretty dubious proposition.

Clearly there are all-stars working for government, and there are schlubs. But the general masses of public sector employees are regular Joes and Janes who want to do a good job. Or, as Metzenbaum puts it in her IBM report: "People and organizations like to do well. Therefore, because measurement enables people to see how well they are doing and adjust their actions accordingly, measurement motivates them to work harder to achieve specific goals even without the explicit promise of reward or threat of punishment."

In other words, the mere act of beginning to measure performance will improve performance. There's no need to attach all the bells and whistles involved in employee recognition or humiliation, although a nice chunk of engraved Lucite on the desk probably never hurt anyone.

So, how might Mr. Huberman apply such concepts to tow-truck drivers? Well, first, he would sit down with the drivers and their supervisors to define some clear markers of good performance. During that process, he and the drivers and supervisors would consider the variety of circumstances under which drivers work, including the variability of the specific jobs they're being asked to do. Once they've established something like a level playing field, *then* they would begin to look at the performance of the different drivers and see who seems to be doing well or poorly.

If someone seems to be doing poorly, then the fair thing to do, of course, is to ask whether outside factors are affecting job performance—particularly narrow streets, a surfeit of "customers" who refuse to stand by quietly and watch their cars get towed away, longer distances to the impoundment lot, or whatever. After that, a good manager might ask whether that driver needs something that would aid work performance (something, that is, *besides* a beater truck that's hit every pothole in the Windy City and hasn't had a brake job since the Cubs won the World Series).

If management has gone through all those basic steps—has asked the pertinent questions about why a certain level of performance is or is not being achieved and has considered all the outside circumstances that might influence performance—*then* chronically poor performers shouldn't be given crummy trucks, a thing that will only demoralize them further and reduce their already abysmal performance. Rather, management should explain to those drivers in the clearest of terms that it's time to start thinking about whether there's some other job—perhaps in the less-demanding world of the private sector—where they might find opportunity and fulfillment.

Of course, the most astute readers out there are probably shouting at this page right now that there's another, more global course of action the city might take: contract the whole tow-truck thing out to the private sector. Which may be appropriate. Or may not. We'll get more into *that* in Chapter 7 on performance-based contracting.

A Lean, Mean, Streamlined Discussion of the Essentials of Performance Measurement

OK now, focusing on results may not necessarily be a popular pursuit in every quarter, but can it be a straightforward one? That is, to what extent can the essential principles and practices behind measuring performance and results be explained in a way that won't leave even the smartest among you geniuses out there wondering what morass you're being led into?

As in *MU1*, this chapter will be devoted to explaining what performance measurement is and how it works. And as in *MU1*, this will probably be the hardest chapter to read (not to mention to write) because of an essential paradox of performance measurement: On the surface, it seems like such a straightforward and commonsense proposition: Figure out what it is you're supposed to be accomplishing and then start charting your performance—whether it's educating kids, protecting the environment, creating safe transportation systems, preventing and suppressing fires, or boosting family and child welfare.

You'd think that these are all policy areas that lend themselves to pretty precise metrics.

The trouble is, the instant you begin laying down a description of what performance measurement is and how to pursue it, it's easy to get sucked into a vortex of arcane terms and complicated descriptions, caveats, and cautions. Just for starters, there *are* legitimate questions about just how much control any governmental entity has over a particular result. But those kinds of cautions should be part of—not an impediment to—discussing what it is government is trying to accomplish (and, not incidentally, what outside or inside partners might be enlisted along the way to achieve certain results).

So, as we get into the key elements of performance measurement, remember that the most important goal is to come up with a small set of good measures that tell you something about your progress in achieving key outcomes—even if you don't necessarily have complete control over that progress. That's it. If you find yourself getting drawn into long debates or discussions about "outputs" versus "inputs," or "outputs" versus "outcomes," try to step back and refocus on the real goal of the activity: assessing the extent to which your work is making any kind of difference in this world.

In *We Don't Make Widgets,* Ken Miller offers a pretty decent rule of thumb for deciding how to focus your search for meaning (it doesn't work all the time, but it's a good start): Try to figure out who it is you're most directly trying to help or serve. The key here is "directly." All public servants are, theoretically, serving society at large. That's great and noble and worth noting. But that higher calling is often built in to the more nitty-gritty jobs being done by government. For example, the gang in the Department of Motor Vehicles does indeed have a higher purpose: to try to ensure that everyone out there on the road knows what they're doing, and that they are tooling around in vehicles that are actually roadworthy. In other words, their big job is keeping the traveling public as safe as possible from harm. But to do that effectively, DMV employees should be providing measurably good service at a very face-to-face level, and by "good service" we are including flunking the occasional granny or grandpa (me included) on their eye test—just so long as the flunking is done efficiently and courteously. There are lots of agencies, of course, that sometimes seem to have dual and potentially conflicting direct beneficiaries—that is "customers"—who they are supposed to be both helping and regulating (even arresting). For example, some of you folks working in departments of environmental protection might balk at the Ken Miller prescription because your job is to directly serve polluters through the permitting process while also directly serving the public by protecting them from the polluters. That's a reasonable point to raise. But presumably if you're doing your job right and well and the laws you're administering make sense (that is, they don't give polluters the right to seriously despoil the environment through valid permits), then you can certainly accomplish both goals simultaneously—and measure the extent to which you're being effective in each, to boot.

Now, as the art of performance measurement has evolved since *MU1*, practitioners have made one pretty important bit of progress: They've more or less settled on an accepted set of terms and definitions. The chief shepherd of consistent definitions has been the Governmental Accounting Standards Board, which has been pushing long and persistently (and somewhat controversially) on the whole practice of performance measurement and reporting. The good thing about the GASB push is that we're moving toward a set of consistent recommended practices (although there are still plenty of jurisdictions doing "grow-your-own" performance measurement efforts, and that's fine). The bad thing about the GASB push is that the material it produces in support of performance measurement and reporting is still about as digestible and decipherable and readable as *Finnegans Wake*. (For you non-English majors out there, take it out of the library and give it a go!)

In fact, though, there are tons of books, pamphlets, and broadsheets on performance measurement, all of them saying roughly the same thing and many of them quite good. If I were to suggest two (OK, three, but we'll set the magnificent tome you're reading aside for the moment) must-reads on performance measurement, they would be the aforementioned Metzenbaum piece, *Performance Accountability,* and Harry Hatry's latest update of *Performance Measurement: Getting Results,* now out in a second edition and published by the Urban Institute Press. Hatry's book can be a head-spinner, too, in parts, but in general it's a thorough and cogent cookbook for how to make this all come together in the real world.

Anyway, the goal of this chapter isn't to be an exhaustive treatise on launching a performance measurement campaign; that's what Hatry's book is for. Nor is it to go into great detail about the critical issue of the psychology of using measures, which Metzenbaum's report does. The goal of this chapter is simply to familiarize the reader with some key concepts and terms in as reader-friendly a fashion as possible, to wit:

Government has always been well known for measuring action, but not what was accomplished through that action. For example, the volunteer fire company to which I belong dutifully and proudly reports the number of calls it responds to each year, typically around 100 or so. Now, this sounds impressive for a bunch of guys who don't get paid and who are extremely busy in their other lives. Kicking off the bedsheets at 4 o'clock on a 10-below-zero morning to respond to an emergency call represents real commitment to the cause.

What we don't report in any detail, though, is what the calls were all about or what was accomplished by responding. To do that would be to reveal the fact that more than half our runs are what we lovingly refer to as "[insert barnyard epithet for bovine byproduct here] calls"—contractors who've kicked off home fire alarms, faulty carbon monoxide detectors, fender benders, backed-up furnaces, phone lines down, and the occasional but regular school kid wondering what happens if he actually pulls the little red handle. (We do have a performance-based motto in our fire company, though: "We haven't lost a foundation yet.")

But we're hardly alone in our confusion (dissembling?) over what represents results. I once was asked by a medium-sized city in the nation's heartland to come out and do an introduction to performance measurement for all the city's department directors. Most department directors came solo, but one arrived with a "team." It was the personnel department, which clearly understood the concept of safety in numbers (of people, that is). As part of the session, I gave everyone five minutes to do an off-the-top-of-their-heads mission statement (if it takes longer, it's either your first day on the job or you're one confused soul).

Herewith the proud declaration of an assistant director of the city's personnel department when asked what the department's mission was: "We do job classifications!" (At this point, a kind of collective groan went up from the other department heads in the room. In talking to a few of them after the session, I learned that the groan was because that *really was* what the city's personnel department regarded as its mission.) When I gently suggested to the personnel people that perhaps their mission was to help attract and retain the best and brightest employees for their fair city, I got glassy-eyed stares.

Meanwhile, a buddy of mine who was hired by a large city to begin laying the groundwork for an ambitious and full-blown performance measurement effort was a bit discouraged at the prospects for the city's child welfare agency when the director declared proudly that simply getting through a two-hour meeting on the topic of performance measurement represented a major accomplishment for program managers. Oy.

But it's a chronic condition that cuts across every policy, program, or internal administrative task, whether it's personnel, child welfare, corrections, transportation, firefighting, contracting, planning, or economic development, and it's easy to understand why. First, it's just easier to measure action than it is results. Second—and related to that—government has direct control over what sort of activities it decides to pursue and so isn't so squeamish about reporting that. But, more to the point, measuring results might reveal some unpleasant truths about your performance that you'd rather remain shrouded in mystery.

(The latter notion is interesting because in reality it's often the case that *everyone already knows* that your personnel department is under the complete control of rule-addled nitwits who take great pleasure in jerking around the very people they should be bending over backwards to help. So don't be so scared about it coming to the mayor's attention.)

But let's set aside the whys and wherefores of what governments do or don't measure for the moment and turn to the dull but vital issue of definitions.

For the purposes of this book, we'll look only at the very basics. And in the interest of congruence or synergy—that is, the hope that we can continue working toward some general agreement on terms—the list of words here and their definitions track the template that experts and institutions like Hatry and GASB use.

Four words and one concept are all you need to understand to get started. Later on you can thumb through Hatry's book and get into more in-depth discussions and models related to the nuances of measurement, or you can visit GASB's Web site for lots of (aforementioned and sometimes tough to plow through) information on the subject of performance measuring and reporting: www.seagov.org/index.shtml.

The four words are: *inputs, activities, outputs,* and *outcomes*. From the standpoint of reporting, the four words can all be considered "performance measures," with each contributing a different kind of information that builds to a more complete picture of whether a particular agency is getting the job done and how efficiently. The concept that we'll cover is *explanatory notes*—the narratives that agencies should be allowed to include, along with the measures, that give meaning to the data. (Explanatory notes, in fact, can go a long way toward allaying the fear that comes with reporting results, as they allow managers to explain why a certain result is what it is, or why it's trending one way or another. This is important because there are certainly times when exigencies beyond an agency's control may be influencing results.)

The trickiest thing about the words involved in measuring performance is that they're the verbal equivalent of quadruplets: They're all closely related, and it's often easy to confuse them, but to be appreciated they need to be recognized as separate and distinct.

The easiest way to explain the four main terms is to fold them all into an example. Let's take the U.S. Department of Agriculture's food stamp program, which is overseen by states and then most often run by either regional state offices or local governments, counties mostly. We'll also use the food stamp program because it's a good example of how quickly what seems like a straightforward performance measurement proposition can get more complicated.

Inputs are the resources expended in the name of the program, including, in this case, things like the administrative and personnel costs involved in running the overall food stamp program, along with the cost of the food stamps themselves. In other words, inputs represent the raw materials that are being burned to fuel the program.

Activities are the actions taken or services provided by certain public employees that turn the inputs into outputs. In the case of food stamps, state or local workers screening applicants for eligibility is an "activity" related to providing food stamps. The main reason governments care about measuring and monitoring activities is that doing so can help tell you a lot about how efficient you're being in delivering those services or taking certain actions.

Outputs are the products delivered through activities. In the case of food stamps, outputs might include the stamps themselves or the number of clients served. Outputs, in other words, are a basic production and workload measure.

Outcomes represent the meat of the matter. They are the metrics that actually tell you whether the inputs burned to generate the outputs delivered are actually having the desired effect. In this case, we're guessing that the desired effect is a reduction in hunger and an improvement in nutrition in the U.S. population at large.

I say "we're guessing" because that's not how the performance of states or localities (or the Department of Agriculture) is measured when it comes to food stamps, which is where the complication comes in.

What is actually measured when it comes to food stamps? Error rates. That is, how often do states or localities give food stamps to people who don't qualify for them, or how often are people given stamps in the wrong amount? States with high error rates are penalized. This is classic "fed-think" and one of the chronic hazards of federal grants programs: Frequently the feds are more interested in the *inputs* and *outputs* side of the equation than the *outcomes* side.

Harry Hatry notes that in this case "performance" actually relates to compliance, not results. As Hatry—who can be brilliant at under-statement—notes: "A compliance perspective can be at odds with an end outcomes–based focus." Yeah, just ask any county child protective service worker how productive a day they think they just had when half of it was spent filling out forms to prove to the feds that a client was actually eligible for services and that all the services provided are documented so that the state or locality can be properly reimbursed.

It's not all bad between the feds and the states, though. For an example of a federal program that's actually made some progress away from simply monitoring how and where money is spent, Hatry offers the early childhood development program, Head Start. A couple of years ago, the feds began to actually track gains made by participating children in learning and social skills—and not just who was getting the money and whether the kids in the program were qualified to be there.

To the Department of Ag's credit, it has been nosing into this territory, as well. It does occasional state-by-state reports on "food insecurity"—a measure of the degree to which access to food is limited by an individual's resources.

Inputs, activities, outputs, and *outcomes,* then, are the basic building blocks of a performance measurement system. If you've got a fairly good understanding of each of those, you're well on your way to being able to apply them to your own job.

Why Did *That* Happen?

OK, let's tackle the concept of *explanatory notes,* which brings us, in-directly, back to the related issues of fear and fear of comparison.

As Ronald Reagan once noted, "Facts are stupid things." It was an interesting paraphrase of John Adams's famous statement, which Adams deployed in defense of the British regulars and officers charged in the Boston Massacre. What Adams actually said was, "Facts are stubborn things." (As for Adams's performance, he won the acquittal of the regulars and officers.)

Actually, facts are both stupid *and* stubborn. They're stupid in that they don't actually tell you anything about why performance is going the way it's going. Why are your streets cleaner? Why is property loss from fires down? Why is turbidity in that stream on the rise? Why are all the kids in the Billy Carter Elementary School scoring in the lowest quartile in the statewide reading comprehension test? Why can't your purchasing department pay a vendor in fewer than 365 days? In other words, numbers standing alone, or set side by side, or one on top of another, or however they may be arrayed, tell you only *what* is happening.

But being "stubborn things," facts are hard to ignore (at least they are if you've started collecting and actually looking at them). Which means the most natural (we devoutly hope) response to stupid, stubborn facts is to do some analysis to explain them.

That's what explanatory notes are for. They are the *why*. If a city is experiencing a spike in crime and simply reports *that* stupid and stubborn fact, the police department, naturally, is going to be open to broad criticism for its poor performance—yet the increase might not really be the department's fault if you start to look at other factors involved. For example, the increase might have coincided with a significant upsurge in prisoner releases, or a significant tailing off in the local economy, or a significant increase in police department retirements. If the department is allowed to look at such factors and report (explain) those along with the raw numbers, then you've not only avoided unfair criticism of the men and women in blue, you've also opened up an avenue for a much more sophisticated and productive discussion about crime and crime prevention in your community and how your community might respond.

Or if some smart-alecky reporter bangs out a story stating that the fire company in nearby Fastville has better response times than in nearby Slowvale, then firefighting officials in Slowvale might be able to use explanatory notes to point out that they cover a larger land mass with the same number of stations, have older equipment than Fastville, and run their department with less man/woman power per capita.

The point is, numbers alone aren't very helpful. What they do is allow you to start asking informed questions about performance and results. They are a jumping-off point for analysis and discussion. The basic goal of any credible performance measurement effort ought to be to stimulate that single question: *Why?* Then policymakers and program managers have the chance to figure out what action or actions they might take in order to improve the numbers or keep them cruising along the right track.

In other words, collecting good data doesn't do anything, in and of itself, to improve government operations. What improves government operations are the questions, conversations, analyses, and debates that are ignited, and then the actions that are pursued once the data start flowing in.

Chapter

Measuring the Unmeasurable

I have a confession to make. For years I've preached the potential benefits of performance measurement for other public officials, while failing to practice it myself. It's not that I haven't thought about it. But try as I might, I haven't been able to come up with any concrete measures for how to gauge the performance of the Ghent, New York, planning board, which I chair.

The planning board handles all kinds of exciting issues—subdivisions, site plans, special permits, and lot-line adjustments. We advise the town board on such weighty matters as subdivision moratoria and revising the town's zoning code. (Just for the record, I get paid the princely annual sum of $1,800 to do this job, so let's not be overly harsh about my performance to the extent that it *can* be judged.) But as long as I've been the chair, I've wrestled with how to assess the job that I and my six colleagues on the board are doing.

The town is in an interesting spot, in both its geography and its development issues. It sits on the high eastern edge of the Hudson

River Valley, about 30 miles southeast of Albany, and is one of those places that used to be predominantly agricultural (dairy farms) but that has been discovered by "city people" as a second-home haven. Meanwhile, farming has fallen off. The overarching document that the planning board consults as it guides the town's evolution from dairy haven to Range Rover playground is the Ghent Comprehensive Master Plan. Like all good comprehensive master plans of its era (early 1970s; we're working on an update) its essence goes something like: "Ghent will encourage growth and development while protecting the rural qualities of the town."

You can see the problem with this right off the bat, right? Do we get points for the efficient, rapid subdivision of Ghent (thereby rendering it no longer rural)? Or are we supposed to somehow put the brakes on development and protect farmland and open space (which stymies the growth and development part)?

Talk to townspeople, and you'll find there's great diversity of opinion on this subject. Those who own land and want to sell it off and move to South Carolina are in the chop-it-up-quickly camp. They think sprawl is a time-tested and perfectly excellent planning concept. Plus, and not unreasonably, they view their failing dairy farms as the equivalent of their 401(k)s. On the other side of the divide, those who have moved to Ghent to escape the congested suburban hell that downstate New York has become are decidedly on the go-slow team. If they see their next-door neighbor walking a boundary line with a surveyor, they are apt to storm town hall with a lengthy petition proclaiming themselves to be "Friends of (fill-in-the-blank)," arguing strenuously that their coveted view ought not to be violated regardless of what our zoning code allows or property rights bestow.

So I called my personal performance priest, Harry Hatry, to confess my long-running sin and get some guidance on what to do. To my immense relief, here is what Harry said: "Planning has always been an area that lends itself less to ongoing end outcomes. It takes so long for the consequences of action to play out, and there are so many other factors that come into play, so in the end you're stuck with a lot of intermediary stuff."

"Intermediary stuff" being things like measuring traffic congestion, perceptions of how the town looks, and general public safety—
all things that over the long run can be influenced by planning-board
action but that are also arguably the result of larger forces, including
local politics, regional economics, and a community's overall DNA.

Certainly we can evaluate how we operate as an administrative
body. In other words, are we doing a good job following the formal
rules and regulations that guide our work? A key measure on that
score might include the frequency with which our decisions are chal-
lenged or overturned (zero and zero on my watch, so far, but we've
got some doozies coming down the pike).

We can evaluate things like the quality of our recordkeeping (we've
moved a considerable distance beyond the brown-paper-bags-in-the-
attic method). And we can pretty accurately judge the extent to which
those who come before us feel that they've been treated respectfully
and fairly—even if they don't always get their way—just by their overall demeanor during and after meetings. (There are always hard cases,
though, which is why my wife still wants me to get the remote car
starter.)

Presumably, if we get clearer marching orders through our updated
comprehensive master plan, the planning board will be able to better
gauge if it is, indeed, performing in a way consistent with town wish-
es. Still, Hatry makes the point that "performance measures don't do
everything" and that planning is still a tricky business. So, if you're a
small-town planning board with a murky mandate, we'll cut you a bit
of slack on the you-can't-measure-what-I-do defense. The rest of you
aren't going to get off so easily.

Prevention

Probably the other most often-cited area that some will argue defies
measurement is prevention. One of the things that people often strenuously assert that cannot be measured is what *hasn't* happened.

In fact, I had occasion a while back to do a morning's worth of
performance measurement 101 for an affluent suburban town out-

side of Boston (actually, there's no longer any suburb of Boston that *doesn't* fit that description). The enlightened town manager, in conjunction with some local resident activists, had grown tired of looking at a town budget devoted to columns of numbers related to tax collections and spending and absolutely nothing else.

What, these townspeople and the town manager wanted to know, was the town actually getting for all of that taxing and spending? Now, you can imagine the delight of all the department heads in this town—who for years had been submitting annual budgets carefully calculated to increase just a tad faster than the rate of inflation—to learn that some pointy-headed journalist was going to be swinging by to ruin their lives by gently suggesting that possibly there was more to the police department's budget than how many FTEs would be funded next year compared with this year.

To my surprise (and I think also to the surprise of the town manager), most department heads actually showed up at the session. We did the usual drill. I explained the basic mission-goals-outcomes-outputs-inputs hierarchy, and then asked them to take a crack at matching those concepts to their own work. And, as usual, everyone in the room struggled first with the very general notion that a budget could be a more strategic document than just how much the town was going to gouge its taxpayers and, second, with the conceptual difference between outputs and outcomes. (An interesting note on this score: in every town or city where I've done this exercise, the library people are the fastest on the uptake and the best prepared. Why? Because for decades library officials *have* actually had to routinely justify their budget requests, and that justification had to go beyond "we just really love books and more of them are getting published every day.")

By far the grumpiest guy in the room, though, was the chief of police. (I have to give him credit: at least he showed up; the fire chief dodged the whole deal.) When it came time to work through the mission-to-inputs hierarchy, the police chief had a simple and, in his mind, fatal question. He was sitting toward the rear of the room, leaning back in his chair, arms crossed, with kind of a weary I-have-so-many-better-things-to-do look on his face. When I asked the assemblage if they had any questions, the chief's hand swung up and he snorted, "How do you measure what hasn't happened?"

Uh-oh, it was the classic you-can't-measure-what-I-do-because-I-do-prevention-and-you-can't-measure-what-hasn't-happened blocking technique, otherwise known as the YCMWIDBIDPAYCMWHH Defense.

If you're a street sweeper, your job goals are clear: To sweep *x* miles of street each day in such a way that those stretches of street may be deemed "clean" by trained observers (or at least by your tyrannical supervisor). If you're a cop, on the other hand, your job is to prevent crime. How do you measure all the robberies, murders, aggressive-driving incidents, muggings, and litterbuggings that didn't happen because you had *x* police officers out on patrol?

Hah, the chief had me! ... along with legions of firefighters (Smoke-Stat), public health officials (Don'tSmokeStat), child protective service workers (BadDadStat), environmental regulators (Don'tDumpStat), restaurant inspectors (SalmonellaStat), suicide hotline specialists (SplatStat), and meter maids (ExpiredStat), all of whose jobs are ultimately to *prevent* bad things from happening, whether it's structure fires or double-parking.

Hatry, in *Performance Measurement*, dispenses with the YCMWID-BIDPAYCMWHH Defense in two succinct pages, pointing out that "the number of incidents that were *not prevented*" is a pretty good stand-in when it comes to measuring the efforts of those devoted to prevention.

For example, one of Tom Frieden's first major initiatives when he took over as head of New York City's public health department was to champion a significant increase in the local cigarette tax, along with a ban on smoking in all of the city's bars and restaurants. In the wake of the tax increase and the ban, there has been a measurable decrease in smoking in New York City (see the New York City *Mayor's Management Report,* at http://home2.nyc.gov/html/ops/html/mmr/mmr. shtml, under "health and mental hygiene"). By measuring what hasn't happened—that is, people who didn't smoke—you've got a pretty good interim measure for the ultimate goal of a decrease in smoking-related illnesses (if not an immediate increase in restaurant receipts). In fact, a recent study out of New York City indicates that smoking is down an astonishing 19 percent from 2002 to 2006, well above the national average, a drop in smoking that experts say could translate into 80,000 fewer premature deaths from cancer and other smoking-related diseases if the smokers have quit for good—not a bad little story about how a government goes about measuring prevention. Now that the city has banned trans fats, it will be interesting to monitor rates of heart disease and obesity—again, the incidence of bad things that *didn't* happen.

But back to our Boston suburb. I'm guessing that what the police chief was hinting at was something to the effect of: Just because there's very little crime in my town doesn't mean the police department's budget shouldn't increase every year. Which is why he didn't like my response to the ultimate question of how you decide what level of resources is right for a department that's in the prevention business, which was: You could do one or both of two things when it comes to connecting the police department's budget and the incidence (or absence) of crime. You could compare yourself with similar jurisdictions, looking at numbers like cops per 1,000 residents or overall law enforcement costs per 1,000 residents, all in relation to crime rates, to see how everyone stacked up. By doing that, you might discover you're spending more for the same results seen in neighboring towns—or you might discover you're actually more efficient. Alternatively, I said, you could squeeze the police department's budget until you noticed crime rates clearly moving upward (we'll call this the Grover Norquist drown-government-in-the-bathtub approach to performance-informed budgeting), at which point you could start adding money back. The chief didn't like either of these suggestions. Shortly after my presentation, the town manager moved on to equally green pastures. The police chief, as far as I know, is still there and still operating on a 1960s model of budgeting and law enforcement. (Meanwhile activity-based costing guru Mark Abrahams tells an amusing tale about an experience with a suburban Boston police chief that *he* dealt with a while back. "After I'd gone through managing and budgeting for results with all the town's department heads, the police chief tells me: 'No way am I doing this managing for results stuff,'" says Abrahams. "Two weeks later when it's his turn to present to the budget committee, he makes one of the most coherent data- and peformance-based arguments for why he needs more police officers that I've ever seen. I'd say he got it!")

IraqStat

So, let's take a moment and consider the hardest job being done by any government in the United States as this is written. If progress on *that* can be measured, then surely little things like social services, economic development, internal personnel practices, or even government's impact on general public health can be measured.

I'd argue that the hardest job that the United States has taken on today is turning Iraq from a dictatorship into a democracy. It's not one that I'd shoulder. It's one that I'd recommend others shoulder. But here we are. And the U.S. Department of Defense at the behest of Congress (Section 9010, Public Law 109-289) is trying to set out clear markers related to progress while we are. The most recent of these reports, *Measuring Stability and Security in Iraq*, offers a host of interesting metrics by which to judge progress in Iraq, ranging from war and insurgency casualties, to crime rates, to business startups, to inflation rates, to rates of oil production, and even assessments of where Iraq is by way of adopting certain key policies.

In other words, if you think you've got an impossible-to-measure mess in your state or city or agency, think again.

Chapter 5

Performance Reporting
The Great Accounting Nerd Food Fight

I f you thought nerds couldn't be vicious, you just haven't crossed the right nerds. Wade into the great performance reporting war, an epic struggle over how governments should report performance—and whether there ought to be established and recognized standards for such reporting—and you risk taking a direct hit in the old pocket protector.

Some background: For many years, the Governmental Accounting Standards Board—the gang that establishes accounting standards for state and local government—has been advocating for something called "service efforts and accomplishments" reporting, or what an editor of mine calls "that service efforts and I-can-never-remember-what-the-'a'-stands-for thing that everyone is fighting about."

What they're fighting about is this: There are certain persistent characters at GASB who don't think that the typical state or local government comprehensive annual financial report (known as a "CAFR" to the accounting cool) actually tells people much about what the government really does and whether all the doing is adding up to any meaningful result. And so this GASB cabal is advocating for some additional annual reporting to add some meat to the bare-bones fiscal view offered by the current annual dollars-in–dollars-out and fund balance roundups.

One part of that addendum would include information related to what sort of action government is purchasing with all the money that is being reported in the CAFR as being spent across all program and policy areas, from social services to law enforcement to public works. These are known in GASBese as "service efforts"—that is, things like the number of needy families served by TANF, or arrests made by the local police department, or miles of road resurfaced that year; actions that would be called "outputs" if you remember all the way back to Chapter 3.

Service efforts, though, only tell you what government is doing and not what results it's achieving through such action. And so GASB would also like to see "accomplishments" reported as well. To follow on from the examples above, an "accomplishment" under "families served by TANF" might include families that have been shepherded closer to independence or that have actually become independent. Related to the output of "arrests," the accomplishments portion of the report might include crime statistics on incidences of murder, aggravated assault, jaywalking, and so forth. Under "miles of road resurfaced" by public works, you might include a subjective evaluation by trained observers of what percentage of roadways in that jurisdiction offers a smooth ride.

Put the two concepts together and you get "service efforts and accomplishments"—or SEA—reporting.

So what's the big deal with SEA reporting, and why have threats of physical and fiscal harm been bandied about in the public-sector-accounting world when it comes to the practice?

Well, it turns out there's a contingent within that public-sector-accounting world (and also within state and local government more broadly) that thinks GASB has no business wandering into this territory—in no small part, they argue, because SEA reporting has nothing to do with financial accounting, GASB's purview.

(Part of the opposition to SEA reporting, though, is clearly also based on reporting fatigue. In particular, governments are feeling beaten up by new GASB accounting standards requiring that unfunded pension and benefits liabilities be reported in government bottom lines. This has elected officials and government finance officers fairly bummed out because of the rivers of red ink that will soon be flowing onto CAFRs. All that is on top of a regimen of fairly recent rules related to reporting the depreciation of public assets—town hall, local sewer systems, on-ramps, and all the paper clips your city purchased last year. And so some government officials will tell you privately that they have no problem with the concept of performance reporting, it's just that they've had enough of GASB for a while.)

Among the most vociferous opponents of SEA reporting is Jeff Esser, executive director of the Government Finance Officers Association. If you want to get Esser's blood pressure up a couple hundred points (diastolic *and* systolic), start asking him about GASB's role in performance reporting.

Esser thinks GASB is the wrong group to be dictating performance reporting standards. "They don't understand the organic nature of government," he says. "When you try to enforce consistency, you may inadvertently and in subtle ways make governments do things that they might not be doing if they decided on their own what to do through a strategic plan and budget."

GASB's response to all this is straightforward: It's not going to force anyone to do anything. Although there was some initial discussion about making SEA reporting mandatory at some point, the gang at GASB has received the message on that score loud and clear and has backed way off. Which is why Jay Fountain, one of the lead advocates of SEA reporting at GASB, now says that GASB is working on "principle-based suggested guidelines for voluntary reporting." Could it be any less mandatory than that?

Now, as I offer my analysis of this whole debate, I have to—by way of full disclosure—note that I once did contribute a chapter to a GASB SEA reporting document. It was a mutually unsatisfactory experience inasmuch as I wanted people to actually *read* the chapter whereas the "editors" at GASB wanted it to put readers into a deep, semipermanent coma. So I can't claim complete dispassion when it comes to who ought or oughtn't to come up with guidelines for performance reporting—GASB scares the hell out of me, too—but not because they might become dictatorial about SEA reporting. I'm more worried that they'll either kick the life out of it before anybody gets excited about the practice, or just confuse people so badly they'll be paralyzed. (Although to be fair, Jay Fountain in person makes a very cogent, tight, and compelling case for the practice.)

What would be nice, though, is if everyone could just quit fighting and simply and mutually agree on some standard practices that state and local governments could follow in trying to report government activity and the accomplishments and results.

Standards of practice would be nice for a couple of reasons. First, they would offer state and local officials some consistent and proven guidance on performance reporting. But they could also facilitate comparison from one jurisdiction to the next when it comes to performance, something we'll get into more in the next chapter. As usual, though, this is one of those instances where emotion seems to be getting in the way of levelheadedness.

But even as the "experts" slug it out, practitioners are proceeding apace, some following the GASB SEA model and some just doing their own thing.

One guy who is moving forward along the lines of the GASB reporting model is Rich Siegel, the head of Bellevue, Washington's budget office. The reason that Siegel is pursuing SEA reporting is simple. He doesn't have any problem with CAFRs as they're currently configured when it comes to offering good and valuable information about fiscal action and conditions in his government. What was frustrating him was the time and effort put into tracking dollars in and out, with no commensurate accounting for whether the money was actually buying anything worthwhile.

And Siegel is hardly alone in his view. "CAFRs are very useful on a certain level," says Michael Matthes, assistant city manager for Des Moines. "But they're not a good mechanism for communicating to the public what they're getting for their money. Just because the dollars add up, that doesn't mean the money was spent well."

Which is why both Bellevue and Des Moines have joined the growing group of governmental entities that have begun to produce a different kind of annual report, documents known generically as "annual performance reports."

The thrust of annual performance reports is to communicate to citizens, the media, and policymakers the real story behind the mind-numbing columns of dollars included in the classic CAFR, by compiling a whole new set of data on what government is doing with the money and whether government activity is resulting in measurable progress.

Bellevue's report, for example, looks at the basics: crime data, the drinkability of the city's water, response times for 9-1-1 calls, and so forth. But it also includes survey data from citizens, asking them to rate the city in broad areas such as "neighborhood livability," and about other basic concerns, such as traffic congestion. (The Bellevue report even asks citizens to weigh in on which of the ratings categories they find most interesting and helpful in order to guide what's included in future SEA reports.)

The Bellevue report is, indeed, full of interesting information. The problem, says Siegel, is that not many people outside government seem interested in it—citizens and the media, in particular.

Part of the problem might be due to presentation. Most performance reports have all the design charm of a car battery. Only the hardest of hard-core public administration jocks are drawn in by the drab pages of charts, graphs, and explanatory notes.

In an effort to combat that syndrome, performance reporters in Des Moines decided to liven things up. As part of the city's effort to actually get citizens to pick the thing up, the city held a contest for local artists interested in contributing to the report's design. The result is *The Art of Community: The City of Des Moines Performance Report*, which displays some really nice work by the locals to lead off the various sections of the report—such categories as "Quality of Life," "Code Enforcement," and "Streets."

Still, no matter how good-looking the annual report has become, Michael Matthes says the *Des Moines Register* typically responds to it with a giant journalistic yawn. To date, says Matthes, the local paper has run only two stories related to the city's report, and they were both lifted directly from it, without attribution or any information about how to obtain a copy of the document. A decade ago, Portland, Oregon, famously paid its local newspaper, *The Oregonian,* for a full-page supplement outlining the findings of the city's first SEA report because the paper wouldn't give the document any ink of its own. That situation has improved, reports Portland's elected auditor, Gary Blackmer, now that some in the local media have become familiar with the report and have developed greater trust in its findings.

Of course, that's one of the most common excuses given by the media for not covering government-produced performance reports: skepticism about governments' self-reported results. The other reason given is, of course, that there are so many other important events taking place out there in the world that the media must cover, such as Rush Limbaugh's tearful admission that *he* fathered Anna Nicole Smith's child (let's hope the kid gets his mother's looks *and* brains). But that's another story.

Anyway, to build credibility, those in the performance-report business note that it's imperative that annual reports include bad news—if the news is indeed bad. "You have to report everything, warts and all," says Matthes.

Carol McFarland, at the Oklahoma Health Care Authority, agrees, noting that the agency's recent annual reports indicate a pretty significant trouble spot. "Child immunization rates are something we struggle with. We're at 72 percent of the federal goal. That's been flagged as an area needing improvement," says McFarland.

Who knows? If government reports bad news, elected officials might actually get into the act and respond. It has happened, says Michael Matthes. When the Des Moines city council got its hands on the city's second annual performance report and learned that the good citizens of Des Moines were unhappy about what they viewed as the deteriorating quality of the city's streets, council members quickly voted to reprogram $6 million toward street resurfacing (and, not co-incidentally, their own political longevity).

Despite the anecdotal evidence that annual performance reports can have real-world value—and ground-level impact—they continue to be a very hard sell. The truth is that citizens and elected officials have, in general, evinced little interest in any in-depth analysis of the actual day-to-day and year-to-year performance of the organizations for which they're ultimately responsible; most elected officials seem happy to rely on that time-honored survey vehicle known as Election Day to gauge broad citizen satisfaction with the job that they're doing, and the minority of citizens who actually get off their backsides to vote seems content with that system, too.

And so government has been slow to adopt performance reporting, either as a matter of homegrown policy or as proposed and outlined more formally by GASB. "I don't think there's probably more than 50 cities that are really doing it," guesses Matthes.

If local governments have been slow to do annual performance reporting, states have gone just about nowhere. Washington is coming on through GMAP, and did publish an initial annual report of sorts (snappily titled *Moving Washington Forward: Holding Government Accountable for Results; 2006 Report to Citizens*). The report is kind of a mishmash of information, ranging from some fairly limited reporting on results to a discussion of the state's efforts to shrink middle management. Even Larisa Benson, who heads up Washington's "stat" effort, concedes that the report isn't great at this point. But it's way ahead of where most states are.

The other state in the reporting hunt is Virginia, with one of the most coherent and user-friendly performance reports in government. The report is available on the state's Web site at www.vaperforms. virginia.gov. And, as will be discussed in Chapter 8, Maryland Governor Martin O'Malley is now pushing hard on data-based governance, and so some good numbers ought to be coming out of his state soon, too.

To inspire more governments to pursue SEA reporting, the Association of Government Accountants is now sponsoring an annual performance-report awards competition. On the downside, winners end up with such grand prizes as no-expenses-paid trips to such garden spots as Schaumberg, Illinois, to receive their awards. On the upside, the AGA does offer some very valuable (and free) guidance to governments on how to do performance reporting, and it also offers extensive and expert critiques of submitted reports to help jurisdictions improve their product (for more information, see www.agacgfm. org/citizen/completed.aspx).

Actually, AGA appears to be helping slowly to create a growing community of performance reporters. But at this point, way too few governments seem interested, and for a host of reasons. The first, most obvious, and most amazing reason is that many in government still don't seem to want to gauge the effects of what they do, much less report it. The second reason is, again, the apparent lack of interest on the part of the general public and the press—and even elected officials (legislators—state and local—in particular).

But I think the third significant reason—and this brings the chapter full circle—is the lack of consistent guidance on reporting. And so a final, desperate, futile plea: Couldn't GASB, GFOA, the National League of Cities, the National Conference of State Legislatures, the U.S. Conference of Mayors, the National Governors' Association, the International City/County Management Association, and the National Association of Counties—heck, might as well bring in the United Nations—sit down and hammer out some parameters or best practices or recognized guidelines for reporting performance?

Wait a minute. If they did that, they might start working cooperatively and consistently on a host of issues, from education to public safety to economic development! Why, they might even be inspired to join forces and take on the feds on a routine and regular basis!

Never mind.

Chapter 6

The Pesky World of Comparison
Or Why Connecticut and Tennessee Are Actually Very Much Alike

You can imagine the surprise of officials in Somerville, Massachusetts, when they discovered that the trash-tipping fees they were paying, compared with nearby jurisdictions, were quite high. You can imagine the trash hauler's surprise when it was discovered that the contract under which it had been gouging the city had never actually been signed by city officials. And you can imagine taxpayers' (pleasant) surprise when they learned that the comparison-based renegotiation is saving the city $700,000 a year over the life of the ten-year contract.

The lesson here? No, it's not that municipal ineptitude can have its occasional advantages (sorry). The lesson is that if you look around a little, you might learn something. And lately, more and more jurisdictions are looking around.

Not that that comes naturally to governments. While comparing oneself to another is almost instinctive among humans, it's not a practice that governments embrace easily. In fact, unless there's some guarantee that the comparison will be flattering, the whole practice tends to be much loathed by those in government.

This is understandable, and for a few reasons. First of all, East St. Louis, Illinois, is never going to be Pasadena, California (unless global warming really kicks in hard). Second, to do any comparisons well requires both hard work and sophistication, and most of the high-visibility efforts that people are familiar with (such as *Money* magazine's livable-cities rankings and *U.S. News & World Report*'s college rankings) are done so poorly as to border on nonsense. And so those being compared are naturally leery about who's wielding the magnifying glass, what they're actually looking for, and just how "what" is being defined, anyway.

The "definition of what" here is critical. So many different governments count things in so many different ways that making fair comparisons can be tough to do. Take, just for one example, the pretty vital crime-fighting statistic of "cleared cases." It turns out that different jurisdictions take a widely disparate approach to how they define "cleared." The most conscientious don't clear a crime until there's been a conviction in the case. Others, though, will clear a case after an arrest. The most creative will dump a stewpot of similar crimes onto one perp—whether there's evidence of a connection or not—and call *all* the cases cleared. So, it's understandable that governments might shy away from standing side by side.

There's a third reason, though, for eschewing comparison that deserves less sympathy. Remember our police chief pal in the Boston suburb from Chapter 4? We all probably had the more-than-sneaking suspicion that he was simply happy with the status quo, and he didn't actually want to step up and see how he was doing compared with nearby jurisdictions because that might mean having to tighten up his ship a little.

The sad and paradoxical thing about that attitude is this: The relatively small handful of jurisdictions that have decided to embrace comparison have discovered that it's potentially one of the most beneficial consequences of measuring performance. When it comes to gauging efficiency and effectiveness, an internal audit can tell you

Activity-Based Costing in a Nutshell

A key element of doing quality comparisons is understanding the art and science of activity-based costing. The great thing about this art and science is that there's a growing cadre of other people who are getting good at this, so you don't really have to.

All you have to do is understand the concept, which, to do a rough equation, goes something like: The cost of any given result equals the cost of all inputs divided by outputs. Simple enough? For example, in education you might divide a school district's total spending by the number of kids who gained a grade that year. The input is the spending. The output is the number of kids who have moved up a grade. The outcome—we presume—is x number of kids who are one school year smarter (that's what standardized tests are for, and that's a whole other story). Yes, it's math at its roughest, but the point is to try to at least link costs and performance.

Depending on how "hard" the service in question is, the math will be more or less rough, of course. Figuring out the per-transaction cost of issuing a driver's license or a building permit is pretty easy. Determining what it costs to educate a kid or rehabilitate a criminal or move a family out of poverty is trickier. Still, there are jurisdictions that are trying to do that.

In fact, some have been doing it for a while; the concept of ABC isn't new. One of the best things I've ever read on the subject is *Costing Government Services: A Guide for Decision Making*, by Joseph T. Kelley, published by the Government Finance Officers Association in 1984 (it tells you how to cost out everything from processing an arrest to maintaining an acre of parkland). Mark Abrahams helped GFOA with an update called *Cost Analysis and Activity-Based Costing for*

continued

Government, which he adds is a bit of a tome. (It's available through the GFOA bookstore at https://www.estoregfoa.org/Source/Orders/index.cfm.) He thinks he and I should do an *ABC for Dummies,* or perhaps for dopes.

quite a bit, for sure. But there's nothing like a field trip or two to broaden one's horizons when it comes to better and smarter ways to do the government's business.

And, in fact, those horizons don't have to stretch really far. Indeed, it's often better that they don't. Take something like repairing potholes. Clearly, Boston doesn't have a lot in common with San Francisco. And so the more politically palatable—and, frankly, practical—approach of close-to-home comparisons has led to a slowly growing phenomenon of regional comparative measurement consortia—groups of governments in the same geographical area that have come together and agreed on a set of performance standards by which each jurisdiction can be measured against the others.

Let's stick with potholes because they are, arguably, the single most powerful indicator of government performance known to mankind and democratic government. At the turn of the last century, Hickory, North Carolina, was flunking Pothole Patching 101, says Karen Hurley, budget analyst with the city. "Pothole patching is a big deal to citizens," says Hurley, "and our numbers did not look good."

Of course, efficient and effective pothole patching is a relative concept. In some places, tossing some cold patch in a hole, rolling over it with a dump truck and then moving on to the next crater is considered state-of-the-art practice. Within a few days, though, the cold patch has soldered itself tightly to the wheel wells of all the tractor trailers that bounced over and then into it, gouging out an even deeper trough (this is known in the business as "pothole recidivism").

The key question, therefore: Who's to say what's good technique and bad? Or when is a pothole really patched?

For Hickory, it's fifteen other municipalities that say what's good and what's bad in that regard. In fact, as part of a sixteen-city comparative performance consortium, Hickory has immediate access to sometimes sobering statistics on its relative performance in a host of areas ranging from road maintenance to fire prevention, and even to such internal functions as personnel management.

And so when assessing the state of Hickory's pothole-patching performance, it was easy to see that Hickory was not measuring up. For example, only 85 percent of the city's potholes were being repaired within twenty-four hours of being reported, compared with the consortium average of 96 percent. (Rather than do head-to-head comparisons among members, most consortia compare to an average, which consortium participants say allows them to see where they stand without the anxiety of being stood up directly against a star member of the group.)

Instead of trying to hide the bad news, Hickory stepped up and used it to analyze its patching tactics versus those of some of the top performers in the consortium. What the city learned was that it was using outdated tactics and equipment. Given the comparative data and lessons in pothole patching from the top performers, the Hickory highway department was able to make a successful pitch to elected officials for a new hot-patch truck.

That Hickory would choose to embrace bad news and use it to improve its performance is probably the key characteristic of the dozens of cities that are now getting involved in regional consortia nationwide. It's still a relatively tiny slice of local governments, though. For the vast majority of municipalities, counties, and school districts, the notion that their performance might be compared with another's is still intimidating enough—or enough of an administrative, fiscal, or political challenge—that they seem to prefer continuing to operate in the comfort of their own small worlds.

Those who've decided to break out, though, contend that the rewards for sharing information on procedures, performance, and costs can pay real dividends.

For example, Randy Harrington, budget director for Concord, North Carolina, says his city, like Somerville, Massachusetts, was able to save hundreds of thousands of dollars a year on a trash-hauling contract by looking at what his city spent on trash collection and disposal versus what other members of the consortium were spending. "We had a big solid-waste contract up for renewal," says Harrington, "and we used the benchmarking information to negotiate that, and it was tremendously helpful on both the cost and the performance side."

Specifically, the city's private-sector waste hauler wanted to jack up per-collection-point costs from $7.07 to $7.76. Concord was able to argue that its costs were already higher than the consortium average and, therefore, was able to hold the line at $7.07. Harrington figures that keeping the cost of collection stable is now saving the city almost $400,000 a year.

That sort of ability to negotiate from a position of knowledge—and therefore strength—has certainly made the $10,000 annual cost of being part of the consortium worth it, says Harrington. "Really, the $10,000 has never been an issue with our city council," says Harrington (Concord joined the consortium in 1999). "But you take the solid-waste example: You've spent $10,000 a year to save hundreds of thousands a year."

Obviously, not all the benefits to being part of a such an effort are so overwhelmingly obvious, says William Rivenbark, director of the consortium, formally known as the North Carolina Benchmarking Project and housed in the University of North Carolina's School of Government (www.sog.unc.edu/programs/perfmeas/index.html). But what Rivenbark says he has noticed since the project got rolling in 1995 is a clear trend in the increased willingness of consortium members to act on the numbers the project has reported. "Of course, that's what the project is all about," says Rivenbark, "using data to improve." In December 2006, Rivenbark's institute released a report, *Benchmarking for Results,* which includes a host of examples of how member cities used comparative data to improve performance, or hold down costs, or both.

It's using data to do things differently that seems to be the sign that a consortium has matured, and in that regard Mike Lawson, director of the mother of all comparative measurement consortia—the International City/County Management Association's Center for Performance Measurement (www.icma.org/main/bc.asp?bcid=107&hsid=1&ssid1=50&ssid2=220&ssid3=297)—says his operation is clearly maturing. "It's the difference between using the numbers to wave a big foam 'We're Number One' finger in the air," says Lawson, "and using the data as a learning tool."

It's not an evolution that comes easily. Comparative measurement consortia are hard to put together and hard to hold together, say those in the business. Changing personnel and changing priorities are just two of the reasons why consortia members may lose interest and drop out. A director of one regional measurement effort compares keeping all his member cities in the fold to "herding cats."

But with the advent of regional and statewide consortia, one problem that has long dogged efforts to create them seems to have been solved, more or less: the old apples-versus-oranges complaint. That is, how can you compare the performance, of, say, St. Paul versus Phoenix, when so much about each is different, from climate to demographics?

That was always one of the more significant challenges for the ICMA consortium, says Lawson. "You have questions about how weather affects one jurisdiction's performance versus another's, or state laws, or whether one is operating in a unionized environment."

In fact, ICMA's project seemed to be stagnating, note outside observers, until the association decided to get into the regional-consortium game too. Now that ICMA is sponsoring regional consortia—there are seven of them at this writing—Lawson says there's been a significant resurgence in interest in the performance measurement program. The number of participating localities—each pays in the neighborhood of $5,250 a year to ICMA—has ballooned from around 120 to more than 160. The consortia ICMA oversees range from Puget Sound municipalities to Virginia counties.

While regional consortia may help alleviate a lot of the comparison concerns, Hickory's Hurley still thinks that being part of a consortium means accepting the fact that no two jurisdictions are ever going to be exactly alike, even if they're right next door to each other. "People say they would like to compare apples to apples," says Hurley, "but how many apples are exactly the same?" Which is why even though her city is one of the smaller ones of her group, she still thinks that Hickory has plenty to learn from larger cities, and vice versa. "I don't care if you have a population of 100,000 or 30,000, the idea is to come away with lessons on best practices."

Also contributing to the growth in consortia, say those who are involved in them, is that a lot of the debates over performance measures and cost accounting have already been worked out; there's more standardization today than there was in the past. At the same time, consortia members argue that the whole notion of measurement has matured to the point where willing participants don't get quite so hung up if there are continuing and hard-to-reconcile differences.

"One thing that our project has confirmed for us is that none of us do the same thing in the exact same way," says Kirk Bednar, assistant city manager for Brentwood, which is part of a twelve-city consortium in Tennessee. "There's just some accepted fudge. Take, for example, the issue of fire department response times. We've gone back and forth on the definition, but it's been a good exercise, and as a result we're doing some things differently." The key, argues Bednar, is to be willing to sit down with other jurisdictions and discuss it all.

Still, significant issues often need to be ironed out whenever different jurisdictions start trying to compare and contrast, even if they both get the same amount of snow every year. Trying to build consistency into what consortium members measure and report, and how each one calculates cost, can prove initially daunting.

Take, for example, the relatively straightforward jobs of paving and sweeping streets. It would seem that coming up with a reliable, multijurisdictional formula for calculating both accomplishments and cost would be pretty simple.

But even that can be messy, says Mark Abrahams, an expert in activity-based costing. Abrahams recently helped a consortium of Kansas and Missouri localities in the greater Kansas City area do a limited comparison project on street paving and sweeping. "We selected those two specific activities based on the theory that they were very straightforward jobs that everyone does," says Abrahams, and therefore, the theory continued, it would be easy to measure and compare among them. "But it turned out far more complicated than we thought. Do you take out a ruler and a map and figure out how far the street sweeper went? Do you measure how long they were out there driving along at eight miles per hour? Do you look at the odometer? How do you account for differences in equipment?" Never mind wrestling with the issues of subjectively assessing performance quality and how each jurisdiction accounts for cost, says Abrahams.

In the end, such issues were worked out, more or less, and participating jurisdictions seemed to get something out of the project. For example, Overland Park, Kansas, beefed up its pothole patrols, and Kansas City, Missouri, adjusted the frequency of street sweeps. Still, says Abrahams, the job was tough enough that it appears to be a one-shot effort for the moment. (Although the exercise has paid interesting residuals. For example, when Somerville, Massachusetts, was looking for a way to do activity-based costing in its public works department, it turned to Kansas City because of that city's already well-developed system.)

All consortia participants concede that there's clearly work and cost involved in the effort, and that a lack of resources—both money and staff—might prevent some jurisdictions from joining up. At that, though, Bill Rivenbark in North Carolina calculates that for a whole city, all it takes is one-quarter of one full-time-equivalent staffer to field the data for all participating departments. But two traits, in particular, seem to characterize jurisdictions willing to join consortia, say those who run them: They have long-standing reputations for being fairly well run, and they tend to operate under council-manager forms of government.

One obvious key to a successful consortium is having some third-party coordinating body to administer the effort. "I think having a third party that doesn't have an ax to grind collecting, scrubbing, and reporting the data is important," says Rivenbark.

The Great Northern Virginia vs. Long Island Government Cost Smackdown: A Parable about Comparison

A recent report out of the Center for Governmental Research in Rochester, New York, offered up a nice piece of comparison, in which it looked at the cost of local government in the Long Island counties of Nassau and Suffolk versus the cost in the demographically comparable northern Virginia counties of Fairfax and Loudoun.

Even allowing for the pesky snow factor, the differences are pretty amazing. For example, when looking at specifics such as per-pupil school costs, the report notes that they are about $18,000 for Long Island versus $12,000 for northern Virginia. One possible reason for the difference, suggests the study: Fairfax and Loudoun are served by three school districts; Nassau and Suffolk are served by (this is not a typo) 127. Another reason for the per-pupil cost differential suggested by the study is that teachers on Long Island make much more money than do teachers in northern Virginia. This raises interesting questions about what, exactly, Long Island is paying for, given that Fairfax County is widely regarded as harboring some of the best schools in the country, whereas Nassau and Suffolk are widely regarded as, well, harboring schools.

In all, northern Virginians spend 30 percent less on local government than Long Islanders, a difference that might be explained by another eye-popping difference in jurisdictional numbers: In all, Fairfax and Loudoun encompass a grand total of nine local government entities. Nassau and Suffolk are home to 439. Consolidation, anybody?

This is not to pick on Nassau and Suffolk. After all, I, too, am the direct beneficiary of New York State's comically frag-

continued

mented gaggle of local governments (remember that $1,800 a year I rake in for chairing my town's planning board?). Rather, it is to note that whether government likes it or not, comparisons will get done—and are getting done. And most interesting and noteworthy is that such comparisons are becoming more sophisticated—along the lines of the center's report—as the art and science of evaluating government performance against cost gets more refined.

So the lesson of this parable: It's better to do this stuff to yourself than have it done to you. And rest assured, it will inevitably be done to you.

But as consortia mature, it's becoming clear that having well-scrubbed and relatively comparable data on performance and cost is only one potential benefit of being part of one. It's the sitting down with peers from other jurisdictions and comparing strategies and tactics that is emerging as another key benefit.

In South Carolina, Anna Berger says the consortium project she oversees at the Center for Governmental Services, which is part of the University of South Carolina (www.ipspr.sc.edu/grs/research.asp), has actually moved away from the annual gathering and publishing of data that characterizes most comparative performance projects. "A year or so ago, we met with our steering committee and they wanted us to add new service areas," says Berger. "It's very time-consuming to create a new set of data and analyze and clean it, and so we're moving in a new direction, away from collecting data and more toward holding local government service delivery forums in specific program areas to share knowledge. So it's more about looking at best practices and less about crunching the data."

But the future of comparison—and its ultimate value to government—clearly lies in the data. After all, jabbering about best practices is all well and good, but probably of much less value if you haven't got good information on actual performance. Even state governments—which seem even more paranoid than local governments when it comes to being benchmarked against rivals—appear to be figuring this out.

For example, a consortium of fourteen states has decided to come together to compare both practice and performance in the whole area of foster care and adoption. In doing so, state officials recognized that, at least when it comes to this particular policy area, Connecticut and Tennessee have plenty in common.

Members of the consortium get regular reports in key areas of performance (to spare states potential political embarrassment, the university blots out the names of all the states except the one receiving the report). And comparisons have led some states to change how they do business. For example, when one of the consortium members—Tennessee—discovered it was lagging in permanent placements of foster kids when compared with the consortium leaders, it did what Illinois had already done, which was to shift to a system of performance-based contracts with all its foster care services providers. Tennessee now ranks among the top consortium performers in permanent placements.

The consortium has been effective enough that it was selected in 2007 as a finalist for an Innovations in American Government award, and deservedly so. In presenting the program to the awards' national selection committee at Harvard's Kennedy School, Fred Wulczyn of the University of Chicago, which coordinates the consortium, said about the smartest thing that was said all day when it comes to the potential use of performance data (and this is a place with a lot of smart people running around it): "We take data and turn it into knowledge."

And so if you and your colleagues are ever struggling to recall the reason why you got into this whole performance measurement quagmire in the first place, I'd suggest you need to do one thing and one thing only: tape Wulczyn's quote over your desk, because the only better saying would be (and here I have the advantage of having just read a bunch of fortune-cookie aphorisms so I'm in the zone): "We take data and turn it into knowledge. Then we take that knowledge and turn it into policy."

Chapter

Performance-Based Contracting

Or Is It a Good Idea to Turn Your Welfare System Over to a Defense Contractor?

Lately there have been more and more stories about all the things that American governments are privatizing, ranging from social services to corrections—even war. Who knows, after governors read the next chapter, they might try to privatize their legislatures.

One obvious reason for this trend to contracting out is that as governments get better at measuring what they do and calculating what it costs, that can naturally lead to the question of whether it might make sense to turn to the private sector to see if it can compete. Can Joe and Moe's Correctional Services, Inc., run your prison system better and less expensively than you can?

That sort of comparison is certainly not a bad thing to do, if it is done in a sophisticated, dispassionate, and thorough way.

The problem is that the whole privatization push has evinced an ideological and political side that seems to have gotten in the way of good and prudent practice—the ideological and political notions being "shrink government until you can drown it in a bucket" and "I'm going to throw as much work as possible to my supporters and corporate buddies as long as I'm in office."

No elected official in recent history embodied the ideological-political camp more completely than Florida's Jeb Bush, who during his two terms as governor launched one disastrous privatization effort after another. (The most recent one to crash and burn was an $89 million effort to overhaul the state's accounting system; it was put out of its misery after Bush left office.)

But a whole collection of other Republican governors, including Mitch Daniels in Indiana, Mark Sanford in South Carolina, and Rick Perry in Texas, are strong proponents of privatizing everything from highways to lotteries. (When George W. Bush was governor of Texas, he wanted to turn over a hunk of the state's welfare system to the defense contractor Lockheed Martin, but the Clinton Department of Health and Human Services wouldn't give him the necessary waivers.)

Of course there are countervailing forces, supported in large part by public employee unions, which hate privatization more or less reflexively. First of all, they don't like that the "cheaper" side of privately provided services all too frequently results from paying those doing the newly privatized work diddly-squat. More to the point, they don't like that privatization reduces the number of government jobs and, therefore, union memberships. They also argue that there's real danger in governments divesting themselves of the capacity to do certain jobs, thereby becoming hostage to the private sector.

They have a point with both the pay and the capacity arguments. It probably doesn't make sense to privatize if the newly privatized workers are going to be paid so poorly that they're eligible for Medicaid and food stamps. As for capacity, South Carolina provides an object lesson: In the mid-1990s, the state almost completely dismantled its own prison-health-care infrastructure, only to be disappointed by the contractor's performance; it took some doing to rebuild the state's ability to take the work back.

On the other hand, there are some good arguments to be made for handing certain jobs off, or at least partnering with for- and not-for-profits in the name of results.

Remember our Chicago tow-truck drivers? Not to mention the Baltimore blacksmith. And if Jiffy Lube can prove it can do fleet maintenance faster, better, and cheaper than public employees, then why not give it a crack at the job? Meanwhile, the whole world of social services is heavily dependent on third-party contractors to deliver a range of services, from housing to job training to substance-abuse counseling.

Which is why whenever anyone asks me if I'm for or against privatization, my answer is always "yes." That is, I'm for it if a *real* business case can be made for it—a business case that includes such factors as the cost of building in-house (or private) contracting expertise and justifying the potential public costs if the newly privatized work pays its workers significantly less money. Which is to say that deciding whether to privatize or contract out takes the sort of sophisticated costing analyses that many governments aren't really capable of.

Even those with some experience in the practice point out that surprises always pop up. For example, when Joe Fistrovich started to get involved in contracting for some basic services for the Indiana prison system while serving as the system's director of finance, he said he discovered very quickly what the state had missed when it wrote its first food-service contracts: that prison kitchens should not run out of food.

While Fistrovich worked out the bugs in the contract, he learned that it's a pretty constant game of give and take—and that the clearer the performance targets, the better. But unanticipated surprises and unintended consequences abound, particularly when the job being handed off is a big one.

That's why what happened in Texas in early 2007 is a cause for real caution in the rush to privatize, but also not much of a surprise: The state canceled its $899 million contract with the consulting firm Accenture, which had been handed the job of doing all the screening and intake work for its child health insurance, food stamp, Medicaid, and Temporary Assistance for Needy Families programs.

When the Texas privatization program was launched in January 2006, it was heralded as the dawning of a brave new era in improved performance at greatly reduced cost. Albert Hawkins, who heads up health and human services for the Lone Star State, was one of the chief and most persuasive advocates of the effort.

But evidence that the business case for social services privatization in Texas had been strongly influenced by consultants who stood to benefit from the whole scheme did not bode well for its longevity. Nor did the fact that the plan was based on eventually dumping thousands of experienced state employees.

And what the state got was pretty predictable—and in fact had been predicted. It got trouble, including such problems as dropped calls, long waits for service, applications not only being lost but actually getting directed en masse out of state, and hundreds of thousands of kids dropped from health coverage for no apparent reason. As I write this, Texas is trying to pick up the pieces. Meanwhile, the media (and certain book authors) are having a field day with the multimillion-dollar fiasco.

The lesson taught by Texas? Governments clearly have to be cautious in pursuing privatization, and the larger the contract, the more cautious they need to be. Before embarking on a contracting-out adventure, they need to do extremely thorough business cases—business cases that are real, credible, and *independent,* and that include an accounting for all the potentially little and big bad things that sometimes happen when governments off-load work.

A significant part of any such business case would have to include one very fundamental component: an evaluation of the extent to which a contractor could be held accountable for clear, documentable performance and results. Absent such a component, it's probably a very bad idea to hand over any kind of work. The same is particularly true if the government considering contracting out has a demonstrated lack of capacity when it comes to negotiating and monitoring contracts. Evidence from the Texas debacle indicates that state officials share as much blame for the meteoric demise of the project as the contractor. (Meanwhile, there is interesting early evidence out of Florida and Indiana that computerizing and consolidating social-services intake can work, but that it works best when public-sector employees are retained to do the job.)

Such privatization megadisasters as Texas's notwithstanding, there is a clear and growing trend within government toward performance-based contracting for all kinds of jobs, large and small. The trend has been particularly pronounced in the children and family services world, spurred in no small part by the federal 1996 welfare reform effort.

The hallmark of that reform was that it put a stop to the federal commitment to supporting welfare as an open-ended "entitlement" (that is, it began time-limiting benefits). That, in turn, put clear pressure on states and localities to begin performing in a whole different way when it came to helping get people off welfare and into work. And because fun runs downhill, states and localities that relied heavily on contractors to provide services turned right around and began demanding a higher level of performance from those providers.

In what still stands as one of the best studies of pay-for-performance in the social-services world, the RAND Corporation a few years ago looked at San Diego County's re-engineered approach to welfare-to-work, post-welfare reform. The San Diego experiment is especially interesting because in trying to key in on best practices, county officials kept some of the work in-house, contracted some to for-profit entities (including Lockheed Martin/ACS and Maximus), and some to the extremely not-for-profit Catholic Charities.

The contracts to Lockheed, Maximus, and Catholic Charities included "pay points"—distinct markers of client progress—for which providers would be reimbursed. According to the report, Catholic Charities performed best, the for-profits next best, and the county third. But what the effort really did, notes the report, is get the county focused on very identifiable and progressive outcomes for transitioning people from welfare to work.

And now there's a term for this practice, one that harks all the way back to Chapter 1. The term is "VendorStat," a catchall phrase for contracting that holds vendors directly accountable for clear results. Again, the social-services world has proved to be especially fertile ground for the practice, in no small part because the old style of reimbursing providers based on caseloads or units of service (rather than

It Works for Roads, How about People?

One program area where governments have figured out the obvious value of performance-based contracts is in transportation construction. In fact, for at least a decade, state departments of transportation have been writing contracts that not only set construction milestones as a condition of payment but that add bonuses for higher performance—which in the case of building (or rebuilding) transportation infrastructure usually amounts to speed.

And so it wasn't that much of a surprise when, in the spring of 2007, contractors in the San Francisco Bay area announced they'd be putting the MacArthur Maze freeway connector, which had been charred and melted in a gasoline tanker accident, back in service less than a month after the incident.

Why wasn't it a surprise? Because the contractor had been offered a bonus of $200,000 a day for every day it shaved off the contracted deadline for the project. Indeed, the contractor netted the maximum $5 million bonus for the job. Given the economic costs of having an important piece of local transportation infrastructure out of service, state officials figured the bonus was more than worth it.

The lessons here? Well, there are at least a couple. The first is that to be confident that the contractor (the low bidder, incidentally) didn't rush the job to the structural detriment of the project, you'd better believe (or hope) that the state had some very tough and observant engineers on the site, signing off on the work. Second, and more intriguing: Could performance bonuses work in other policy and program areas, such as social services?

continued

Some jurisdictions that are doing pay for performance in social services, for example, do increase reimbursements for services to clients who are recognized as needing more help than others. And New York City is in the process of launching a program that pays parents for good parenting, including attending school meetings and taking their kids for regular medical checkups. The $50 million pilot program is being funded through private donations and is modeled after a similar program that has been operating in Mexico City for a decade. The theory, of course, is that it's cheaper to invest a relatively small amount of money in encouraging socially and civically responsible behavior *now* in return for potentially significant positive social, civic, and economic outcomes down the road.

So how about a performance bonus—say, $200,000—to every contractor who helps shepherd a family off of welfare and into documented independence, if the family remains self-sufficient for at least five years? It might just be worth a pilot, too.

on results) frequently set up a fundamentally backwards incentive structure: Providers ended up financially better off keeping clients *in* the system than lifting them up and out.

The state of Illinois figured that out when it started to notice something very troubling about its foster-care system. Like a lot of state and local foster-care programs, the state relied heavily on not-for-profit providers to manage caseloads. And, as with a lot of state and local foster-care programs, providers were reimbursed based on the size of those caseloads. Bigger was better, at least from the standpoint of a provider's bottom line. In other words, when it came to Illinois providers, permanent placements in a good home—the whole point of foster care—would mean the provider earned less money.

The result of that sort of perverse incentive system? Caseloads in the mid-1990s in Illinois ballooned almost 150 percent in just over five years. Illinois had more kids in foster care per 1,000 than any other state, and the length of time kids stayed in foster care was increasing. And so Illinois did something smart and interesting. The state got together with its providers and worked out a whole new system whereby the providers would be rewarded not for carrying crazy caseloads but for placing kids in permanent homes. The results of this new approach were impressive and predictable: Caseloads plummeted, going from 49,000 kids in the system when the program was launched to 26,000 three years in.

When bureaucrats start to focus on the right data, all sorts of interesting things can start happening. For example, there came a point in the 1990s in Oklahoma when officials overseeing job training and placement of disabled citizens didn't like what they were seeing: It was costing $22,000 per case and taking more than a year to place people.

And so the Department of Rehabilitation Services began experimenting with what came to be known as "Oklahoma Milestones." Under the new system, providers (those doing training and job placements) were paid in stages: a certain percentage upon client evaluation, a certain percentage for successful completion of training, a certain percentage when the client got a job, and then increasing percentages the longer the client stayed on the job. To prevent creaming, the department upped reimbursements for harder-to-place clients.

In all successful cases of a VendorStat approach, proponents note that fashioning a system that builds in new, more rational incentives and that is fair to all parties requires working closely with both providers and clients (and their advocates).

So, you'd think this grand experiment in performance-based contracting and focusing on outcomes would be sweeping the nation, right? Trading e-mails with a friend who oversees a state association of county social-services directors, I asked her if her folks were doing much in the way of performance-based contracting. She said no, in part because her members are still struggling with which outcomes to use in gauging performance. But the other reasons her members were continuing with the status quo (fee for service and caseload counts, basically), was that the county departments were so starved for resources that they couldn't come close to paying for the sort of expertise that would be required to do a good job of negotiating and monitoring performance-based contracts.

But clearly, governments *are* starting to figure out how to ensure that they get real results for the money they invest, even if some continue to lag in implementation. (Just imagine the transformation in programs and operations if privately run prisons were reimbursed based on recidivism rates!)

So, the lessons from places like Illinois and Oklahoma are pretty simple. Performance-based contracting can be a powerful—even transformative—tool for getting tough jobs done more efficiently when all parties are clear on what represents performance and results.

Still, if you really want to make splashy headlines and get people talking, then experts strongly recommend continuing the old-style "best-guess" and "high-hopes" model of contracting out—more formally known as "WhoopsStat."

Chapter 8

Elected Officials (City Councils and State Legislatures, Especially)

The Weak Link in American Government?
Or Will They Ever Measure Up?

Not long ago, a friend sent me an amusing clip from the *Los Angeles Times.* It was all about how the city had been sending out notices to thousands of residents telling them that their dishwashers hadn't been inspected as required by city statute. And, indeed, the city has at least one guy who travels around town looking at and under dishwashers—mostly dishwashers that were installed long ago and have worked just fine, thanks—and signing off on them.

They say that it's tough to watch laws and sausage get made. That may be, but at least what comes out the other end at a sausage plant smells and tastes pretty good.

So one can imagine the kind of ingredients that might have gone into this link of, er, sausage in L.A.: The niece of a city council member circa 1989 witnesses the "great deluge" when her improperly piped dishwasher disgorges soapy water all over her kitchen floor. Let's say her name is Mary Ellen. Mary Ellen steps forward to shut the thing off and is summarily electrocuted because the dishwasher wasn't wired properly either.

Next thing you know, we've got a city council member hammering away at the necessity of a "Mary Ellen's Law" to protect the unwary dishwasher purchaser-installee from a similarly grim fate. The unions representing plumbers, electricians, and the city's various building inspectors jump on the bandwagon. And before you can say "Whirlpool," the city has passed its inspection law … and it's pretty much ignored thereafter. That is, it's pretty much ignored until the city's elected auditor notices the arrears in inspections and cracks the whip.

OK, I completely fabricated the part about Mary Ellen and her council member uncle and how the inspection requirement became law. But the parts about the city requiring all dishwashers to be inspected and the city auditor's decree are both true. Meanwhile, we do know that there was never an epidemic of catastrophic dishwasher failures in L.A. to trigger such a law. But it's a good bet that there had to have been some incident or interest group that at some point lobbied and inspired the L.A. city council to do what legislatures are very good at: making sweeping law based not on good data but on good anecdote or political expedience.

The craziest thing about the L.A. story, though, isn't so much the law as it is the response to the city auditor's findings: No one in L.A. city government is questioning the requirement. "Managing and Budgeting for Results 101" would dictate that someone on the L.A. city council ask the city's building inspectors or public health officials or fire department to pony up stats on the relative threat posed by mis-installed dishwashers in order to gauge whether this law ought to even stay on the books. But no, the push is to narrow the inspection backlog.

OK, here's a completely true and scary performance-based story from the Golden State that I witnessed with my own bespectacled eyes.

A highly competent and resilient upper-level bureaucrat whom I got to know in the course of covering state personnel issues for *Governing* was handed an interesting and worthwhile assignment a few years back: The state of California's corrections department was pushing hard to bring more women in as corrections officers. As part of that push, the department instituted a thorough and aggressive effort to train all corrections officers in what constitutes sexual harassment. Not only that, the agency created a clear and easy-to-access system for reporting incidences of sexual harassment. Then it strongly encouraged employees to use it.

So what do you think happened in the wake of this concerted effort?

(a) Reported incidences of sexual harassment plummeted because all the male corrections officers were so shocked by the revelation that for years they've been acting like sexist knuckle-scrapers that they all immediately decided to become sensitive new-age guys.

(b) Reported incidents of sexual harassment took off like a Saturn V rocket.

(c) Our game bureaucrat was publicly raked into the coals by the chairwoman of a Senate committee "investigating" skyrocketing reports of sexual harassment in the state's corrections department.

If you answered (b) and (c), then you've got a pretty good grasp of the relative statistical literacy (and political instincts) of a good dollop of elected policymakers in the United States today.

That's right. Our bureaucratic hero was flayed by the oversight committee's chairwoman at a public hearing because in the wake of the new sexual-harassment awareness and reporting regimen, reported incidences of sexual harassment went way up.

I tell this story a lot, and a number of friends of mine who are in very strong positions to judge aren't surprised by it, nor are they encouraged by what they see when it comes to state legislatures or local elected councils on this particular score.

But I'm an optimist, and I say that there are pockets of progress—even what some might characterize as enlightenment—and, therefore, some cause for hope as that dedicated mass of legislatively inclined out there grinds out sausage, bratwurst, and *krakowska podsuszana* in their never-ending effort to legislate us into some new and happy order.

To wit: As an alderman in Somerville, Massachusetts, in the late 1990s, Joseph Curtatone was perpetually frustrated by the budgets his board was supposed to be helping shape and approve. "Budget time really used to get me," says Curtatone. "It was a straight line-item budget. There might be a small paragraph for each department briefly describing what they do, but there was nothing that told you how much we spent on what—no inputs, outputs, or outcomes."

It was classic best-guess budgeting, characterized by one imperative above all, says Curtatone. "If you're the DPW director and you come in and have $15,000 left in your account, then that's how much we cut your budget by for next year," says Curtatone. "And so the message to all our departments was 'spend down your budget.'"

Anyone who has witnessed public sector budgeting close up is familiar with the imperative. If you wander into a state or local government office and notice a pile of yet-to-be-unboxed computers collecting dust, you can make a pretty good guess at the late-in-the-fiscal-year frenzy that went into purchasing them.

But the budgeting business was just one of the major points of the alderman's frustration. Curtatone was also amazed at how the city went about managing money in general. "Here we were, a multimillion-dollar operation with absolutely no real-time information on even the most basic services. We weren't measuring anything. How many potholes were we filling? How were we filling them? Which departments are racking up overtime and how much?"

The simple fact that Curtatone harbored such frustration made him an odd breed of elected legislator. Other elected policymakers with some experience to draw on agree that Curtatone is the exception to the rule. When asked to comment on the average city council person's familiarity with the concepts surrounding results-based budgeting and management, Indianapolis city council veteran Jackie Nytes lets out a long sigh. "Theoretically, if I ask city council members if they're in favor of using data to make decisions, they'll say, 'Of course.' But a lot of that is just lip service."

The fact is, council members seem to be much more comfortable "trying to micromanage departments because it's easier and takes less time," says Nytes. So rather than have an in-depth discussion about program and project funding in relation to what the city is trying to accomplish or what citizens want, Nytes says council members are more likely to focus on something minutely concrete, like trying to reduce the number of cell phones being used by city officials.

"A lot of council people are part-timers, and so it's a challenge," says Nytes. "It's not that they don't want to or they're not capable of it. The fact is, making budget decisions based on information about results is just harder."

But if her counterparts around the country are going to deal effectively with delivering services in times of tight resources, she thinks the way to do that is elevate the conversation. "If we're really going to get a handle on budgeting, then the question shouldn't be, Do we have enough money for this many jail beds? The question should be, Do we have the programs in place so that we don't need so many jail beds? If legislatures are acting responsibly, then they should be focusing on those kinds of outcomes and not trying to manage every little thing themselves. That's what city employees are paid to do." (The sound you just heard in the background is a loud and definitive "amen" arising from a vast army of frontline city employees from coast to coast.)

To the extent that legislative bodies do start taking a serious look at outcomes, it often is because of tight budgets—or budgets in a certain area that seem to be spiraling out of control.

During the 1980s and 1990s, for example, legislators across the country took part in a great race—to see who could be toughest on crime, otherwise known as the "lock-them-up-and-toss-the-key" school of criminal justice.

In pursuing this race, few of the hard-charging legislators ever asked for an analysis of cost in relation to potential benefit (one state was an exception: North Carolina, which came to its senses earlier than any other state because corrections costs there already were beginning to spiral out of control).

In the wake of the get-tough spree, a growing number of legislators are noticing little things like: "Gee, my state is now spending more money on corrections than on education, and the costs are showing no signs of slowing." And they're deciding that's not such a good thing.

And so some big states are starting to rethink how they do criminal justice. As Alan Greenblatt points out in a *Governing* feature story (www.governing.com/archive/2007/mar/prisons.txt), California actually changed the name of its Department of Corrections to the Department of Corrections *and Rehabilitation* (what a concept!). The reason: 170,000 inmates and billions of dollars in expenditures later, some geniuses in the state legislature (along with the governor) started figuring out that the state's corrections-spending path was, as we put it in public sector fiscal-speak, "unsustainable." And so maybe the state should start thinking about how to prepare inmates for release, and how to support them once they're out so that they don't make return visits.

See Dick and Jane Make Law; See Law Fail While Driving Costs to Moon

It's not that there aren't people out there trying to help legislators make this conversion from largely emotional actors to more rational ones.

For example, the National Conference of State Legislatures now offers *Legislating for Results,* an apparently not-so-best-selling publication that was a joint effort of the conference and the Urban Institute. The book and accompanying CD are aimed at beefing up your average state legislator's performance-based literacy (the CD, presumably, is especially helpful for those legislators who don't read).

Legislating for Results isn't a bad book. In fact, it's really a pretty good primer on all this stuff, and I recommend it. What's a bit scary about it, though, is how basic it is. It seems to assume that those coming to the subject (that would be your average state legislator) not only lack a fundamental understanding of statistics, cause and effect, and trends tracking, but also a clear understanding of the legislator's role in governance—not to mention a lick of common sense.

Of course, except for the most dedicated and curious of state legislators, few are going to plow through dozens of pages of pretty dry material on performance measurement, so the package that NCSL sends out includes a bookmark entitled "ASKING KEY QUESTIONS." And, to be safe, the KEY QUESTIONS are printed on both sides of the bookmark (see bookmark, page 84).

But if state legislators have been a tad slow on the uptake, might local elected officials be sharper? Perhaps. Indianapolis's Jackie Nytes is part of an effort sponsored by the National League of Cities that is aimed at coming up with a similar *Legislating for Results*–type tome for local elected officials.

As chair of the league's CityFutures Public Finance Panel, Nytes is part of a team working with performance measurement guru Harry Hatry at the Urban Institute to produce a manual and other materials that she hopes will encourage local elected officials to stop micro-managing and start focusing on a bigger, more performance-informed picture.

In the wake of *Legislating for Results* and because of the buzz around performance-informed work done in states like Texas, Louisiana, Washington, and Oregon, Judy Zelio, who follows fiscal affairs for NCSL, thinks there has at least been an uptick in interest in information on legislating for results.

And some out there in the field can testify to that. Mike Marsh, deputy director at the Oregon Department of Transportation, says it has historically been something of a mixed bag when it came to what legislators seemed to want to focus on when his department presented data on goals and outcomes. Recently, though, he says he's noticed more focus. In fact, in recent discussions with the chairs of the House and Senate budget committees in Salem, officials from his department were told to be ready to directly link dollars and outcomes. "They also said that if requests for additional money weren't related directly to key performance measures, don't even bother asking," says Marsh.

Meanwhile, says Marsh, the committee chairs seem to be holding their own folks accountable for familiarizing themselves with ODOT's facts and figures on costs and accomplishments before *they* come to the budget hearings, as well.

But getting legislators to really buy into legislating for results has never been easy. I was in Austin back in 1998 to interview then-Gov.

George W. Bush because it looked like he was going to run for president. In the course of doing some supporting interviews, I had occasion to visit with a legendary legislator and budget wrangler, Senator Bob Bullock. At the time, Texas was being held up as a model of performance-based budgeting, and I asked Bullock about that. "Aw, that's just window dressing," he said. According to Bullock, the legislature knew from experience which agencies were doing a good job and which weren't.

Certainly some legislators have enough institutional memory and familiarity with the state's agencies to make some informed judgments about their performance. But especially in an era of term limits, and as line agencies become more technically adept at measuring what they do, more advocates of data-driven government are arguing that more than an agency's reputation for good or bad work ought to go into the spending equation.

All this isn't to say that there aren't some good reasons a policymaker might be uncomfortable using data to make big dollar decisions. After all, state and local agencies of all sorts have on occasion been known to produce a foodstuff of their own commonly referred to as "fudge"—which, come to think of it, is about as good for you as sausage. For example, the Houston school system caused a ruckus when it simply decided to underreport truancy. And there was quite a dustup when New York's subway cops at one point tried to lay a bunch of their bad numbers on the beat cops up on the street.

The potential for agencies to produce numbers that, to be generous about it, might not have solid footing in reality is an understandable phenomenon, especially if we think all the way back to Chapter 2, "Crime and Punishment," and our discussion of actual, everyday uses of data. Do legislators use data to inform discussion and decisions or as a blunt object with which to smack around bureaucrats?

To the extent that the temptation for creativity will always be an issue, it would certainly help legislators to gain confidence in the whole managing and budgeting-for-results thing if they knew they could rely on the numbers.

Which is why it is important that auditors be an integral part of the process (for those of you who are hopelessly addicted to this stuff and so actually *have* a copy of *MU1*, all of Chapter 7 is dedicated to this and is entitled: "Key Principles of Public Management: Lying, Cheating and Bumbling").

If auditors aren't brought in early to help fashion measures, chances are they're going to pop away at them from the outside. Which happened recently in Maryland.

In theory, at least, Maryland has been doing something like performance-informed budgeting since 1997, when it embarked on what it called its "Managing for Results" process. According to the latest legislative auditor's report on the practice, "MFR was introduced to agency leadership as a strategic planning process to help officials set goals, objectives and performance measures for programs and to assess the results of those programs." The auditor's report (which, not incidentally, was undertaken at the request of the chairs of the Senate and House budget and appropriations committees) noted some key reasons why the program might not be as effective as it could be.

For one thing, the report states, the number of measures reported to the department of budget and management was closing in on an astounding 9,000 for sixty-four state agencies. At the same time, the audit report noted that the executive branch itself had been doing a routinely poor job of linking budget requests with agency goals and results. Most critical, though, the report found that almost two-thirds of agency-reported data simply was not verifiable. It's not that agencies were making the numbers up, necessarily; it's just that auditors couldn't confirm them as accurate.

Despite the report's findings, Maryland Senator P. J. Hogan, who serves on the budget and tax committee, contends that he and his fellow committee members do pay close attention to the link between money and key results when they make budget decisions. "I find that MFR works very well for me as a budget person. I can look at an agency's budget and look at their goals and see how they're doing and make a better judgment as far as whether we're getting the right amount of bang for the buck," says Hogan. "Take a measure like infant mortality rates. Under our MFR guidelines, we can look and see what it was in the four previous fiscal years and at least see trends—hopefully going in the right direction. And if not, then we can say, 'Hey, this program is not working, let's pull the funding.'"

Meanwhile, the executive side of Maryland government is promising to tighten up its MFR act under Governor (and former Baltimore mayor) Martin O'Malley. O'Malley is taking the principles and tactics he practiced in creating and administering Baltimore's much vaunted CitiStat and is applying them to Maryland through "StateStat," kissing cousin to Washington Governor Christine Gregoire's "GMAP," discussed in Chapter 1.

Even as legislation was pending to make StateStat official during O'Malley's first legislative session, he was already pushing it in three key agencies: corrections, juvenile justice, and social services. Senator Hogan doesn't see StateStat as either bolstering or overriding MFR. "I see it as complementing it," he says.

While elected officials like Hogan—and certainly O'Malley—are clearly past Budgeting for Results 101, Hogan does concede that most other legislators in Maryland probably have only passing familiarity with the whole MFR regimen, because they are less focused on the budgeting side of legislating and more into "establishing new programs."

Connecting Stats and Citizens—The Next Frontier

Despite the continuing state of general ignorance or indifference among legislators when it comes to using data to make important decisions, the ranks of governments that are turning to more results-based programming and budgeting seem to be slowly growing, frequently because two or three people, like Curtatone and Nytes and O'Malley, become frustrated enough to try to shoulder their jurisdictions in a new direction.

For Curtatone's part, he took the most direct route possible to that position of influence, running for mayor of Somerville. Upon taking office in January 2004, Mayor Curtatone promptly organized a series of field trips to Baltimore for top staff.

The result was "SomerStat," which he says is now standard practice in his city. "For the first year, our aldermen were saying, 'Oh, yeah, SomerStat, explain that to me again?'" To ease the board into the program, Curtatone's early budgets had both line items and performance-related costing. Now, he says, using data to discuss budgeting has become standard operating procedure.

What hasn't happened in Somerville yet, says Curtatone, is taking the information being collected on government performance and results and pushing it out to citizens so that they can be more tuned in to what's being accomplished with their tax dollars. That's the city's next big step, he says.

Some elected policymakers, like Indianapolis's Jackie Nytes, think that taking the data to the residents is the best reason of all for making a clear connection between dollars and results. She says one of her most significant objectives in working with the Urban Institute on producing primers on budgeting and managing for results is to change the conversation that elected officials are currently having with taxpayers.

"Revenues are getting tighter and tighter, and we're not going to micromanage our way through this," says Nytes. "We have to reframe the discussion with the taxpayer. This isn't about looking for fluff in budgets, for waste. We're already efficient. The question is, Are we efficient at the right things? So this is about what we want to budget for—what are our priorities and what do those cost?—and then explaining to citizens the tough choices: If you want all these services, then you may need to increase taxes to pay for them."

One elected policymaker Nytes wouldn't have to work hard to convert to her way of thinking is the new head of the finance committee in Somerville, Maryann Heuston, who has served on the board of aldermen for seven years. "We are accountable to the people who put their good, hard-earned money into taxes, and this allows us to show them what they're getting for it," says Heuston. "This is about openness and transparency."

Heuston notes that having detailed information about spending in relation to results has flat-out given her more confidence as an elected official and has really tuned her in to what's going on around the city. That, she says, has allowed her to engage with citizens in a much more open and productive way.

And, in the end, that may be the key concept here. Lately, more states and localities seem to be figuring out that keeping constituents in the dark about what government is spending money on and what it's accomplishing through that spending is a formula for continued distrust and skepticism (and smoldering tax revolts). As Jackie Nytes noted, and as dozens of other public officials are figuring out, governing intelligently and responsibly is becoming less and less of a top-down, black-box exercise.

So perhaps as part of any state legislative or local city or county council swearing-in process, officials should not only pledge to uphold the Constitution, but also commit to "turning data into knowledge and knowledge into policy." And then they can buy themselves a good book to figure out what, exactly, they just promised to do.

Index